when the night bird sings

when the night bird sings

JOYCE SEQUICHIE HIFLER

COUNCIL OAK BOOKS
TULSA / SAN FRANCISCO

Council Oak Books, LLC
Tulsa, Oklahoma 74120

03 02 01 00   5 4 3 2 1

CATALOGING-IN-PUBLICATION DATA
Hifler, Joyce.
      When the night bird sings / Joyce Sequichie Hifler.
                  p.   cm.
      ISBN 1-57178-096-3
      1. Hifler, Joyce.   2. Cherokee women—Biography.
      3. Cherokee Indians—Social life and customs. I. Title
      E99.C5H66   1999
      814' .54—dc21
      [B]   98-50271
                                        CIP

BOOK DESIGN BY CAROL HARALSON
COVER DESIGN BY SHANNON LASKEY

To my husband, Charles J. Zofness

To my daughter, Jane Hifler

To my Friend and Counselor, The Holy Spirit

. . . and to all the Night Birds in my life.

when the night bird sings

acknowledgments

THE AUTHOR WISHES TO ACKNOWLEDGE with deep appreciation the friendship and help of the late Mildred Milam Viles, daughter of a Cherokee chief, who supplied a quantity of American Indian quotations from her extensive library in Claremore, Oklahoma.

Portions of this work have been taken from the author's nationally syndicated column, "Think on These Things."

The Cherokee words and phrases are phonemic translations from the Cherokee Syllabary that was given to the Cherokee people about 1821 by Cherokee genius Sequoyah. Several dialects change the spelling and pronunciations.

foreword

SWEET SPARKLING NOTES ARE GIFTS of the
night bird. A musician of high clear places, the night
bird copies everything it hears. It sits atop the highest
tree and replays what it has heard to all who will
listen. It mimics even the baby chicks as they follow
the mother hen among the grasses, across shallow
streams, and under porches.

   Meadows are sweet with the soft sounds of
doves and coo-coos, and the bobwhite calls "where
are you?" to its covey. Meadowlarks wearing yellow
bibs and black necklaces pour out their uninhibited
songs in the sunshine. Deep in the dark forest an owl
chuckles in its daytime sleep, and crows try to stir up
trouble with constant cawing.

The song of the night bird, or mockingbird, cuts through all the other sounds and finds the ear of the poet. Ordinarily the mockingbird is a daytime singer, but it is not uncommon for the mockingbird to record too many songs. Once in a while, when all is quiet in the velvet darkness, a sudden burst of music fills the night. Rare and brief, the night song strikes a high vibration, and in the twinkling of an eye something or someone is changed dramatically. A change not earned — coming by grace alone. Grace, the unearned favor which makes us ask what we did to deserve a certain thing.

Nothing, nothing at all. It was the love-gift of the Great One.

Listen quietly . . . and hear.

when the night bird sings

PAPA TAUGHT ME how to shoot, Uncle Carl taught me how to cuss, Grandmother E lis i taught me how to gather herbs and greens, and E li sti, Cherokee Mama, taught me how to pray. It was the latter that saved me.

"You are a Cherokee, and you are a Sequichie. Act like it."

Such words cover a multitude of rules for behavior, and I lived by them.

Mama in Cherokee is E li sti. My mama's nickname was Gyp, short for Gypsy, because she had dark skin and green eyes.

Mama was afraid of nothing. Not of dogs — the neighbor's dog, Bingo, bit everybody in the neighborhood except Mama.

Not even of snakes. As we walked to the mailbox each day, we had to go over a rocky hill where I gathered little round rocks to put in the rock garden. One day, Mama saw a huge blacksnake crawling up over a bank beside the road. She said "You know, I always heard a person couldn't pull a snake backward. I wonder if it's true." I started yelling because I knew she was going to try it. Sure enough, she grasped the snake's tail, braced her feet and tried with all her strength to pull it back toward her, but to no avail. Finally she dropped the snake's tail and brushed the dirt off her hands. "Well," she said, "They were right."

Her strength amazed me. I saw her put a splint on a young heifer that had fallen and broken a leg. Most farmers would have said the heifer had to be destroyed, but not Mama. She held that heifer down, put its leg in a splint, and it lived to bear many calves.

After I'd had a tonsillectomy Mama was sitting with me in the hospital when several wreck victims were brought in for emergency treatment. The hospital was short on staff so she was drafted to help out. She worked for hours helping to set broken limbs, sew up cuts and bind up wounds. When he heard about it later, Papa said, "Well, I didn't know they could ask someone to help that was not a nurse." Uncle Carl said, "This hospital brings in people to sweep for a couple of days and then calls them nurses. Gyp's a nurse."

But those same hands that wrestled with snakes and set broken bones did delicate needlework. Most of the time we embroidered and Mama tatted lace with nothing but thread and a little celluloid shuttle. She worked long at her little Singer pedal sewing machine and was a genius at cutting her own patterns and making my school clothes out of hand-me-downs. Any little scraps of fabric left over were knitted into rugs or stitched into beautiful quilts.

Mama was strong-willed and self-sufficient, traits which helped her raise me and many of her sister's children. Aunt Nina had ten children and Mama provided a complete layette for each one as they came along. When my cousin Es went to college, Mama made her clothes. A lot of love went into the things she made, as well as work. And she prayed for all of the children, too, as they grew up and went away to school or to war.

Mama also wrote a news column for the *Nowata Star*. One item that she wrote said, "The Yorks transacted business in the city this week." But when type was set, it turned out, "The Yorks ransacked business in the city this week." Uncle Carl never let Mama forget how she insulted our good neighbors.

Many young men and many nephews lived nearby and all of them had great respect for "Aunt Gyp." She saw my cousin Bus and his friend Bill York slip into the shed one day but she said nothing because they came right out and left without a word. After they were a safe distance away, she went to the shed and found a half-pint of whiskey hidden. She knew they were attending a party that night. Mama emptied half of the liquor from the bottle, poured water into it and returned it to its hiding place in the shed. Many years passed before she admitted what she'd done. "Weak whiskey!" Bus said after her confession. "And we thought we could really hold our liquor. We didn't even get a buzz!"

I grew up believing Mama could do anything. She had a second sense about many things. She could find lost articles and often found nests that setting hens and guineas would hide in the woods.

I was playing in the rock garden one day when I heard a drone. As it grew louder and louder I made a dash for the house. When I told Mama what I heard, she said, "Oh! It must be a swarm of bees!"

She left the sewing machine, ran to the shed and brought out an old tub. Then she found a heavy stick, and began beating the tub with it.

"Shout as loud as you can!" she told me. "We are going to settle those bees!"

We made enough noise until one by one they began to settle on a tree limb. Soon there was a round ball of crawling, humming bees around the limb. But we did not have a hive to put them in, so gradually, they flew away again. Honey for biscuits would have to wait until we found a bee tree in the woods. Still, I learned how to settle bees should I ever decide to be a beekeeper.

By the same practical methods that she used to

settle bees or remake hand-me-down dresses, Mama taught me to pray. From Mama I learned early that prayer never fails — unless there is no faith at all. She told me about the time I was a baby and had diphtheria. The doctor told her I would not live through the night, but she wouldn't accept such a negative edict. She prayed through the night and I was cured. She never told me and I never asked, but I have a feeling that in those prayers she dedicated me to the work I am doing — and the Great One honored that request.

I learned from Mama that the true church is within each of us, and it is a personal responsibility to keep it orderly and to worship there often. I have not forgotten. I go there every day.

ELISI,
GRANDMOTHER

ELIS I WAS MY FRIEND. Wherever she was, I was right behind her — and it was often in the woods gathering greens and herbs. She always wore a hat and in early spring she would remove it so I could fill it with wild Easter lilies and pink striped grass flowers. I picked a plant called sheep sorrel, which we children called "seep showers." It had a wonderful tart flavor and, with a little sugar sprinkled on the top, it gave me a little taste of sweet.

Grandmother was a tart little woman as well. She wore her gray hair knotted on the back of her head and she sewed long modest dresses with tiny lilac flowers or a gray print.

I don't suppose she ever had a cream for her hands and they were work-worn and rough, but I thought she was beautiful. She knew how to use home remedies, often massaging kerosene on my aching legs to warm the muscles and ease the pain. She also made a broomweed tea that tasted awful. I tried never to be sick with anything that required broomweed tea.

My grandmother was a mass of contradictions. She was a believer and tried to keep what the preachers taught, but she had a streak of orneriness that I know I inherited. She tried to keep the Sabbath holy and would not let me go to a baseball game on Sunday. I hated being left behind when my cousins were all going, but even then I was aware that I was a loner — not belonging to the close-knit families of cousins.

On the other hand, Grandmother could shock and she especially loved to shock one woman she called the "church lady." I never knew why she felt such animosity towards the church lady. I watched her sewing a black-and-white striped dress for herself and I asked if she intended to wear it to church. I knew very well that wearing such a bright dress to church would be considered a sin.

"Of course," she said, "and if the church lady says anything, I'm going to tell her I think I look like a striped-assed ape."

I took her comment with a grain of salt, but I should have known better. We were attending some function at the school house and Grandma had on her beautiful black and white dress. Here came the church lady. She gushed over the dress and I heard my grandmother say, "I think I look like a striped-assed ape."

End of conversation.

E lis i taught me that words could be the strongest medicine of all. When I was feeling haggard or ugly, she would tell me, "Speak to yourself. Tell yourself you are fine looking, and everything around you will agree and want you to be happy."

Grandmother kept my grandfather Sequichie's memory so alive that it seemed as if he was always with us, even though he died four years before I was born. He had sat for a portrait at some time or other and we had his picture. He was a full-blood with black hair combed smoothly back from his high cheekbones and prominent nose. His eyes were black and so bright they seemed to snap.

I grew up hearing stories about my grandpa, how he played the fiddle, preached sermons in Cherokee, and translated Cherokee law books for non-Indian courts. I was told he stood for wisdom and strength in the neighborhood.

No one ever admitted it, but I know he must have played fiddle for a dance or two — though that would have been discontinued when he converted to the Christian faith. In those days, Christians weren't supposed to dance. The Indians were looked on as heathen because they danced, just like King David in the Old Testament was reprimanded for dancing before the Lord. The Cherokees had always danced before the Lord and sung in high-pitched voices. Despite how it looked to the Christians, they were a reverent people.

They saw God as the source of all good things and they earnestly worshipped and gave praise. Later, the Christians would decide they could dance in worship services, too, and many of them would throw reserve to the wind. In the early days, however, Christians thought dancing sinful, so once Grandpa converted, our family did not dance.

My grandfather began to preach in the Cherokee language and his followers were devout and faithful. During the flu epidemic of 1917 he went from house to house attending sick people and praying for them. None of the people in the church offered to help, but a prostitute went along. Without worrying about catching the deadly disease themselves, Grandpa and the prostitute worked relentlessly to help the sick and dying.

Only a few doctors were available to treat the ill, but with the technology of that time there wasn't much doctors could do anyhow. Cherokees had always believed in healing the sick through prayer, and that didn't change when Grandpa converted to Christianity. He used prayer to bring about healings that changed peoples' lives and gave them new reason and purpose. He believed that more would have been saved if they had only known the Word and learned to rely on it before they fell ill.

UNCLE CARL

HE WAS DEAR AND GENTLE AND KIND — and ornery if he saw anything or anyone being hurt. He looked amazingly like pictures I have seen of Geronimo. And he was an unmerciful tease.

Red and Jude were a beautiful pair of mules that Uncle Carl owned. They were sleek, leaning more to the horse mother than to the donkey father. But like mules, they tried his patience; they'd wait until he walked up to put a halter over their heads and then they would kick up their heels and race off over the hill. One day I shuddered to see Uncle Carl come out of the house carrying a shotgun and walk resolutely toward those mules. Surely he would not shoot Red and Jude! But when they turned to run away as usual I saw him lift the gun to his shoulder and a shot rang out over the hills. Red and Jude stopped in their tracks but they didn't fall dead. Uncle Carl pointed to the barn and shouted, "Red! Jude! Get in there!" As he stood there pointing, the mules turned, ran to the barn and disappeared inside. I couldn't stand it, and I ran down to the barn to see the blood and examine the wounds. There was no blood, just a few tiny welts raised up on their rumps where they'd been stung with the light bird-shot Uncle Carl had put in the shotgun shells. From then on, all he had to do was shout to those mules and they obeyed.

Uncle Carl would never really harm an animal. He was the person everybody's dog went home with. It nearly broke my heart the day a man in the neighborhood shot a dog and just left the injured animal to suffer and die. Someone came to Uncle Carl who lived a short distance away and told him the dog was crying and dragging its hind quarters. Uncle Carl quietly took his gun and went down to finish the job. He put the dog in a burlap sack and went to the man's house and knocked on the door. When the man opened the door, Uncle Carl said, "This is the dog you hurt and left to die. If anything like that ever happens again, it will be you in this bag." With all his might, he flung the bag back into the man's house and walked away. His word was not doubted, and nothing like that ever happened again.

PAPA

FIRST HE WAS AN UNCLE, and then when he went into the Army Corps of Engineers during the war, he became Papa. He had always been my father figure, but when he went into the service, he legally adopted me so that I would receive a support check from the government. The check was a godsend, though it only amounted to a little over eight dollars a month. Up to then, our income had been limited to farm produce.

Papa was a big Cherokee, weighing something over 230 pounds. He wore a size twenty shirt and a size fifty suit. His one necktie had extensions in the middle so that the tie would hang down past his chest. He was a good man, very honest, and he had a wonderful sense of humor.

Although his talent was not considered to be his best asset, he was tremendously gifted. He could sketch a picture without one erasure. He built furniture and put it together with pegs. My daughter still treasures an oak library table Papa made, so sturdy that it could be dropped out of an airplane and not come apart. Before the war, School District 36 hired him to design and build school bus bodies. After the buses were in operation he drove one of them for thirteen years before going to the Engineers.

Another of Papa's talents was communicating with young Indian men from the hills who hardly spoke English and who lived much like our ancestors did, back in time. The Engineers put him in charge of a company of Indians from all tribes in an effort to teach them white man's idea of military discipline and the ways of army authority.

Papa told the story of one particular man who never let on if he understood how to show the respect due an officer. While walking on the parade ground one day, he and Papa suddenly came face to face with a captain. The officer stopped to stare at the man, waiting for him to snap to attention and salute, but the Indian merely jerked one hand out of his pocket, waved, and said, "Hiya, Lieutenant!"

Upon his return from Engineers, Papa was hired by the State of Oklahoma to supervise a truck crew on the highway. In postcard to a friend who lived only a mile down the road, I wrote how glad we were to have him home. Mama was shocked when she read the message, "Papa has turned into a highwayman." She took time to teach me the difference between being a highwayman and having a job with the State Highway Department. Soon Papa was hired in a more reputable job as undersheriff for Nowata County.

He was well fitted for law enforcement because he was not afraid of anyone and he was willing to do whatever was required. He was apt at "sensing" a problem and taking charge of it without delay, and he knew the ways of the northeastern Oklahoma hills. He could sniff out a still whenever the wind blew the particular smell of sour mash through the trees.

These were prohibition days and there were many cars running whiskey from wet states into dry Oklahoma. He would catch them, sell the whiskey back to the wet state and sell the car to benefit the State of Oklahoma. Before such sales were legal, he would bring all the confiscated liquor out on the sidewalk, systematically break the bottles and let the whiskey flow down the gutter and into the sewer system. This was not a hard task for him since he as a teetotaler and he had no problem with the "waste." But people came to watch the spectacle and a couple of men asked, "Sheriff, would you care if we got down and drank some of that out of the gutter?"

"Go ahead," said Papa. He did not believe they would actually do it — but they did.

When the sheriff retired, Papa was elected sheriff. He held the job for twenty-seven years. He was always on duty, always available, and widely respected by the law officers and by those he served. People relied on his generosity. One woman called Papa when her cow was sick and another asked for help because her chimney was stopped up. He delivered death messages, cooked food for the prisoners.

Once when a woman was murdered Papa helped with the autopsy. The bullet had gone into her forehead and not come out, but it was needed for evidence at the trial. The coroner had the unpleasant job of sawing the top of her skull to get the bullet. When he got tired, Papa was called in to finish the job. The bullet was retrieved and the murderer was convicted.

Since Papa was a sharpshooter, he was called to do unusual things. Once some men came to the office to get him to go into the river bottom to hunt for a cougar. They had found its tracks when they were hunting and did not want to go after the cougar alone. He told the men that it was summer and hot and there would be many insects and tall weeds. But if they would go catch the cougar they could tie it to the mailbox in front of his office and he would look after it for them. The men went away shaking their heads, no cat was ever found, and the flowers around Papa's mailbox bloomed in peace.

Folks in Nowata still tell stories about Papa's sense of humor. A man who worked for Papa in the sheriff's office told me about a time he saw Papa's 230-pound bulk behind a sapling that had recently been planted in front of the bank building. As the man approached, Papa jumped out and drew his (unloaded) pistol. "Stop that! You'll scare someone," the man said. Papa told him, "No I won't, because I'm hiding behind this tree. And besides that, nobody can see me because I'm an Indian."

It was Papa who taught me to shoot. He would throw a stick into the rock quarry, which was full of water, and when it popped up I was supposed to shoot it. He told me to hold steady, to use my natural instinct, and he added, "Make the gun a part of yourself."

Our family was rich in love and humor and personality. Summer nights we would all sit together on the front porch in total darkness and tell ghost stories, snake stories, and stories about unusual events and supernatural lights. I can still hear the mosquitoes humming, and I remember how someone would check the direction of the wind, then build a small "smudge" to drive the insects away with smoke.

On moonlit nights, Mama would take all the children on a hike across the prairies. We usually found a haystack to slide down, and then we'd go home with chaff in our clothes. Those hikes brought family and friends close and gave the boys something to recall when they were away in the war.

Bus went to Egypt, Johnny to the Fiji Islands where he was friends with the Fiji chief.

And we stayed home — Mama E li sti and me. We worked and we prayed until finally our prayers were answered, the war ended and the family all came home again, safe.

A PLACE
OF PEACE

THE BARN HELD ALL MY SECRETS, all my pains, all my fears. It was in this place that I could be myself and talk to the Great Spirit without reservation. Built of native timber, the barn had silvered and stood as a sanctuary for me and for the cows that came down from the hills in the evening to be milked.

A shallow stream rippled over the rocks to the south of the barn. There were times when rain peppered down on the roof. If it rained a lot, the water would run riotously over the rocks and roots, foaming into round clumps in the deepest part of the stream. I loved wading there, though it meant walking on the smooth rocks in the bottom of the branch — and if I slipped on the moss and fell, so much the better. It was as close as I could get to swimming.

At the end of the day, I would put out fresh hay for the cows and the sweet smell of it brought them through the broad door on the south to stamp their feet and feed while I did the milking. Gracie the cat came to beg for a taste of milk and I could never resist squirting it into her pink mouth. She was soft and gentle, a good companion for this special evening hour. But she would hear mice in the granary and leave me to investigate.

How pleasant it was to sit in the barn on a milking stool when my chores were finished and listen to the whippoorwill. Once in a great while an owl would awaken in the oak grove to the west, and his song would quaver in the twilight in tones so primitive and sweet that it hurt to listen. Every person who had lived here, walked here, or found solace here seemed to be a part of the owl's serenade.

My mother's voice carried clear through the evening air, saying, "Supper!" I loved this time of evening. As I walked up the beaten path to the house I could see the lamp light and it meant security and love. The barn had been my sanctuary — and would be again when I shed tears over a young man who wanted no ties to hold him as he prepared for a long stay in the air force.

I see now that I was being prepared for a life that would not always be easy.

Science and technology have changed many things since those slow, sweet beginnings. I never dreamed the world would take such giant strides and I would be carried with it. But none of the modern technologies can bring me the solace I found, and still find, in the natural world.

Nature is the original, upon which all else is patterned. All of our inventions have been derived from this essence, this blueprint of the Great Spirit.

TO HAVE
AND TO HOLD

CAN YOU SEE THE WIND? Can you touch the love shared by a family? Is thought visible? Is it possible to see what brings overnight miracles every spring?

One man said he could believe if only faith could be tangible — something he could touch and grasp in his fist. But most things worthwhile are invisible — love and peace and inner well-being. We can't see these things, but their results are evident. We search for them every day. We cry for them. Ironically, the only way we can have them is to be open and receptive in the belief that we already have them.

What we see with the physical eye is only a tiny part of life. Mega-life exists on the invisible plane. If our spiritual eyes were suddenly to open we would see how near the answers are to our questions.

We waste our time questioning and asking for proof of something we already have, the grace of life. We can claim this miracle with our words.

The miracle is there, why not draw it in? You cannot earn it, I cannot earn it, but when we believe and refuse to say negative things, the Spirit knows and delivers.

TIMES WERE HARD. Summer drought had ravaged the land, the well had gone dry, the chickens no longer laid eggs and the cows gave no milk for lack of grass in the meadows. But water was a necessity for drinking and bathing. Mama, in her usual efficient manner, set out to use what was at hand to get it.

A half mile or so from our house was a hand-dug well that always had water. It was situated on low ground and was probably spring-fed. Mama made a sled out of scrap lumber, loaded a barrel on it, and harnessed the horse to pull it. We were off to get water — but it had to be drawn up bucket-by-bucket to fill the barrel, and this was no small effort.

Our Cherokee allotment land lay in the crest of three hills. Almost everything that had anything to do with our lives was played out on those hills. Storms, when they finally came, would come from the west. The school bus came over the north road, and coyotes slipped over the east hill in sly efforts to catch one of our hens. Other things happened over the east hill as well. British cadets were making training maneuvers there, diving and turning as though they were in combat. With Papa away in the Engineers, stationed in Virginia, Mama and I were on our own — so much of my time was spent riding my horse, Figger, over the east hill where everything could be observed.

The hill was not a particularly friendly place — except to snakes, hawks, and rabbits. All I had to do was walk across the pond dam and I would be at the base of the hill. There were many trees around the hill, but my favorite was a wild holly with red berries. Though I was not allowed to eat the berries, the birds loved them. The lower limbs of the tree drooped down to the ground giving me a hidey-hole when I needed it. Bread and butter and green onions made a nice little picnic for my dog and me, away from anyone that might want to intrude. (Of course, no one ever did.)

I was on intimate terms with every other part of our land, knew it like the back of my hand and loved it as my very soul. Like all Cherokees, I felt that the land was a part of me. It was integral to my spirit, from the wet-weather streams with sandstone bottoms to the huge ash trees and elms and the lush wild strawberry beds that hugged the sides of every moist ravine. Like a house painter uses two different paints to decorate, the Decorator had used two different stones here. There was limestone on top of the east hill and sandstone at the bottom. What truly amazed me was that two different rocks could be so near to each other and never together. I courted and wooed the hill — invited it to be my friend — and it ignored me like the sought-after girl ignores the young man in pursuit of her company.

The east hill was unlike all the others. I rode my horse at full speed across all the others because they were free of rock, except for a few flat limestone boulders that were white in the twilight and shied the horse unexpectedly. Whenever that happened, we would stop and check out the strange enemy. Soon Figger was quiet, and I'd hear him pull at the prairie grass, and it would squeak through his teeth.

But the east hill was not hospitable to Figger. Here thick slabs of limestone lay flat and only inches apart so that even my foot could not fit between them.

There were no expanses of prairie grass, only a few wild persimmons growing here and there and clumps of wild pink verbena. Even these few isolated flowers looked like they had a temporary foothold among the great limestone boulders. More times than not I was barefoot and it was impossible to walk on the rocks because of sharp fossils that proved an ancient sea had once covered the hill.

So many complicated things for an Indian child to understand. Why did everything have to be so hard? Why did my mother not have the things she needed?

In a way, the hill told me. Life had its hard places and its comforts. It had flowers and cactus — sometimes a rainbow and sometimes a storm cloud. But I had love, my mother, my horse and my dog — and I had these hills.

When drought-breaking rain clouds finally came that summer, they found me there, on the east hill. As I turned back toward home, the raindrops that fell on my face mingled with tears of gratitude.

FLOWERS

WHEN I LEAVE THE HOUSE IN THE MORNING and walk through the garden, I cannot help but think how these flowers, these plants, these bits of bright color are simply basic Truth. Flowers are thoughts of the mind, colorful ideas we can cultivate. Flowers are people we know, too.

In the dead of winter these flowers are not dead. They wait for warmth, wait for the season to bloom, wait to be cultivated — and then, they give us something equal to forgiveness — and they give us peace and love.

As much as I love these flowers, it pleases me to leave the well-tended beds of bright color to roam freely over the hills and glens to see the wildflowers. Wildflowers have not had attention. Instead, they have had to overcome the extreme harshness of snows and drought and having been trod under the feet of cattle. They exist simply because they have power in their tiny seeds to germinate and multiply. I see spiky wildflowers with rough exteriors and herbs that heal, but the delicate and beautiful blossoms are there as well. The violets that bloom in shady places along a moist creek bank and beneath fronds of mayapple are delicate beyond belief, yet they bloom in ironclad profusion. They let nothing stamp out their main goal — to flower, to perfume, to add something beautiful.

When I take the time to look for and cultivate Truth, I realize I am part of a garden where blooms never fade.

PICNIC ON
ANDERSON CREEK

EVERY BLADE OF GRASS GLISTENED, every bird-song was a concert, every shaft of sunlight was the warmth of heaven. We were going on a picnic — just Mama and me.

The very idea of a picnic was exciting to me, but where it was to be held was even more wonderful. Mama and I would ride our horses miles back into the ranch pastures to a place called Anderson Creek. But we had to get there first, and all of the journey was something to enjoy.

We left early in the day. I was riding Figger and Mama was on Maude, a gentle mare with a white star just below her forelock. We carried with us a jar of water, a skillet, matches, a blanket, a wash cloth, and some aspirin. These basics were never to be forgotten, Mama claimed. But I also took a small pail of milk. Mama said we didn't need it, but I insisted, so it was tied on my horse.

We rode through the woods and saw wild flowers and squirrels and heard the cardinal sing. We followed a wagon road to Big Creek where we crossed at the ford — a gravel ridge in the creek bed with a foot or so of water spilling over it. We paused for the horses to drink and then rode up the wagon road to higher ground. Here our best farm land gave up Indian arrowheads when it rained.

Soon, we were out on level pasture land where the trees thinned and we could see long distances. This is where I saw my first fairy circle — a large circular growth of toad stools, and I was so excited I yelled, "Mama! Look at the stoode toles." She laughed out loud, because I would reverse my words whenever I was excited.

Most people call these toad stools mushrooms because they look the same as those we see in grocery markets — big white globes on stems. But I had training in what to eat and what not to eat in the wild. Certain berries were forbidden and I knew that "crow poison" can look very like wild onions. I knew how to avoid toad stools and jimson weed.

A while later, when it seemed to me we should be there, eight or ten horses emerged from the far woods. At first glance I was afraid, because range horses usually tried to fight the horses we were riding — nipping and kicking sideways. We spent a lot of time trying to scare them away. But as the horses came closer, we could see there were men on horseback, and this was not a pleasure ride for them.

Mama said calmly, "That is a posse. They must be looking for someone."

They turned in our direction and as they approached us we could see they were armed. Their horses snuffed and stamped their feet as they rode up to us.

"Have you seen anyone walking or riding along your trail?"

Mama assured them that we had seen no one, and she asked, "Who are you looking for?"

"We are searching for Pretty Boy Floyd. If you see anyone give us a whoop or ride and catch us. Do you know if there are any caves or cabins around here?"

"There are none that I know of," she told them, "but over that way is a well that may or may not be covered. I have not been there for awhile."

They thanked us and tipped their hats, and we rode on toward Anderson Creek.

I asked Mama why she told them about the well, because no one could hide in a well. She told me they thought someone may have killed the outlaw and dumped his body.

Pretty Boy Floyd was forgotten as soon as I saw the swing. We came to it just before we got to the opening of Anderson Creek. Many years before, someone had used cable to make a gigantic swing in a tall tree. I loved to swing but it always made me sick to my stomach. No doubt someone named Anderson had built it and I was grateful, even if I couldn't take but two or three "up-and-aways."

When I caught up with Mama she was already standing down by the creek.

It was beautiful. Crystal clear and spring-fed, it was shallow but wide and had a gravel bottom. The water was so cold I could not comfortably wade, but we did refill our jar — and there in the creek was our picnic; dozens of large crawfish crawled in the clear water.

Mama built a small fire and I opened my milk bucket to drink. To my surprise, the bucket contained butter. The jiggle and jostle of the horse had churned my milk to butter. Mama laughed. "Butter and no bread. Well, we can cook our crawfish tails in butter."

When the fire was burning down to large coals, she reached into the creek and lifted out a crawfish, nipped off its head and claws and dropped it into the simmering butter. I was amazed to see it turn bright orange. She lifted it out of the skillet and laid it out to cool, and then she gave me instructions on how to eat it.

"Break off the tail and turn it over. When you break through the shell, you will find delicious white meat."

I did what she told me and was ready for more before they had finished cooking. In later years, I would savor my first taste of lobster. These large craw-fish had the very same wonderful flavor. So there we sat, an Indian woman and her little girl, deep in the wild, outlaw-infested hills of northeastern Oklahoma, picnicking on "lobster" cooked in fresh-churned butter. But there was more to come.

We started toward Big Creek and saw evergreens in every height and shape. We made mental notes so that when we were nearer Christmas, we would be able to ride back here and haul our tree home.

But suddenly our horses balked. Their eyes wide and wild, they pranced and rebelled against going any farther. Mama said in a calm voice as she patted Maude's neck, "There is a rattler somewhere near." Then Mama started to dismount.

"Mama, stop!" I protested loudly, but she was already busy scrutinizing the road ahead and alongside. She handed me Maude's reins and told me to be quiet, then moved toward the rocks.

"Here it is," she called at last.

I heard large rocks thumping on the ground time and again.

"Got 'im!"

She came back, took Maude's reins and led the way back to the snake. Figger and I followed. The rattlesnake was coiled up near the water's edge, and, though dead, was still writhing, its rattles still moving.

For Mama, it was not good enough that she had killed the snake. She was determined to take it home for the rest of the family to see. She tied a slender rope around its bloody head and dragged it home behind her. Snapshots still exist in family albums for posterity.

After all these years, I wish that I could take my husband, Charlie, and my daughter, Jane, to see Anderson Creek. But I am afraid I may have built it out of proportion in my memory and it may not be as grand as it was when I was five or six.

No, it is just as grand. It is too far back in the hills for litterers to find.

UNCLE

ONE THING that could not be contradicted, this young man was an Indian. Straight line mouth, straight black hair, high cheekbones, and an ornery spirit that was challenging and creative to the point of aggravation. He was a miniature Geronimo with a sense of humor and of the mind that people should be bullragged beyond their endurance. It is said that as a young boy he put on his father's spectacles that had no lenses and turned to look intensely at the dog. He said quite seriously, "Rover, I can see your guts." Scolding did little good as he went from one thing to another with a clear conscience and a sense of enjoyment.

One day a baby girl was left in his care while the mother and grandmother worked in their garden. She was up and about — toddling one way or another, and he was weary of the constant chase. A little thought brought a creative solution. He sat the toddler down and tied a rock to her dress tail. Her squalls and howls brought Mama and E lis i from the garden and he was told in no uncertain terms to stop mistreating the baby. Then the women returned to the garden.

But even a small child can be remorseful, and the little girl's love for him was so adoring she could not bear to have him scolded. Without the slightest hesitation she went to him and pointed to her dress tail and the rock. Please, Uncle, tie it on again if that is what makes you happy, she implied. Suddenly the rock was unimportant to her, because the love would last a lifetime of lifetimes.

CHRISTMAS
LOVE

EVERY SEPTEMBER we began saving anything that would decorate a Christmas tree. We had no lights, bulbs, or plastic of any kind, so all during autumn we laid aside little bottles, pieces of foil, burr acorns. Then, near Christmas, Mama and I would ride miles to select and bring home the best evergreen we could find in the woods for our Christmas tree. Here we'd lovingly hang our collection of treasures.

I loved sitting on the warm pine floor behind Grandmother's wood range to play and listen to Grandmother sing "Beulah Land" while she made homemade sausage for Christmas. Above my head were shelves of homemade plum jam that I always hoped would turn into chocolate. It never did. But I loved to put my hands on the resevoir of warm water at the end of the range, and I loved to hear her putting food in the warming oven above the burners. Wood smoke is still perfume to me and different kinds of wood made different fragrances. Many times, Grandmother and Mama would leave containers of milk out on the wash stand where it would freeze on very cold nights. One of them would spoon out the frozen cream from the top of the milk and add sugar. This "ice cream" was a treat for me, even in the coldest weather.

And it was cold. When I was five, heavy snows came two days before Christmas. Mama took great pains to explain to me that we had an exceptional amount of snow — so much that even Santa might not be able to get through. But I knew Santa Claus and I knew he would make it, no matter what happened. I wanted a doll and a blackboard, and Mama assured me that Santa would get me what I wanted — as soon as the roads were passable. Did Santa need a road, I wondered? I didn't think so. After all, Papa could still get his school bus out, even though many of the school children could not get to the bus stop.

Christmas Eve came and Mama put me to bed early. Everyone seemed so happy that night, that I couldn't imagine Santa not coming. I could hear Uncle Carl laughing and telling stories as he loved to do. I tried to stay awake and listen, but my cozy featherbed felt so much like a cocoon that I imagined myself like a little caterpiller hibernating before its transformation into a fancy flying flower. The voices in the kitchen faded into my dreams.

I woke Christmas morning to the fragrance of frying sausage — my favorite. Mama came in to get me and she said happily, "Santa Claus came. Come and see what he brought."

There was a doll with red hair and eyes that opened and closed. Oh, how beautiful it was! And there was a blackboard with an eraser. I couldn't write on it for a while because the paint still needed to dry. But I loved the chalk and the little set of tin dishes I had not even asked for, but wanted very much.

Christmas was the gift of all gifts when I was five, and it still is. I never hear "Silent Night" without thinking of Mama. Even to this day we sing together in spirit. I know that on that snowy Christmas so long ago, Papa found a way to get the doll and the dishes. Probably he went to town in the school bus over the snowy roads. And Uncle Carl painted that blackboard for me. Hard times? Maybe. But these were beautiful times, full of love that means Christmas to me, even to this day.

REASSURANCE

THIS MORNING, I shuffled my feet through the loose leaves on the path to the woods and felt the last wintry days weighing on my spirit. Spring has never failed to come, but these final dreary days are cause for impatience.

It seems that as we get near to a goal, time shifts down to a lower gear and tries to make us believe we'll never reach it. But as I knelt beside a decaying log and pushed my hand spade into the loose soil in search of the first tender green onions, I heard something. At first it was the faintest of sounds, but so strangely familiar that I stopped to listen intently. I heard it again. This time no doubt existed. I scrambled to an opening in the trees and looked up at the sky.

Everywhere I looked I saw silver wings turning in the sun — and again, that unforgettable cry of wild Canadian geese in their northward flight. Nothing has ever been so primitive or so new as the sound of geese.

Somehow, in those brief seconds, my attitude was transformed. Spring was coming.

And then, I saw there in the rich earth the first tiny threadlike shoots of wild onions poking through.

I knew and was reassured, not only about spring but about so many other things I had questioned in my heart.

How amazing that I would need to be reassured of something that has never failed.

From the great to the very small, I see the Creator's handiwork, the shine on a leaf, the intricate petals of the first flower in spring, the cry of geese — even my own heartbeat — and I still ask to be reassured.

SUMMERTIME WAS ALL THINGS LOVELY TO ME. No school, no shoes, no cold weather. But sometimes it also meant no rain.

One summer after the well went dry, I heard my grandmother say to my mother, "We may have to take some rough weather to get a good rain."

Storms frightened me. When they came, E lis i would grab the old tin match box with all the important papers in it and we would run through the orchard to the cellar. Sometimes the sky would turn a greenish-yellow and we would stand at the yard fence to watch for cyclones. Even though the storms were partially hidden behind the rolling hills and prairies, we could see the threatening, angry clouds boiling high.

One time a young neighborhood girl stood there with us. "I'm disappointed," she said, lightheartedly. "I thought we would see people and houses and things going up in the clouds."

"No, honey," my mother told her, "that is the Rapture, when God rescues His people from harm's way."

As we watched the storm move along the horizon, a funnel dipped down from the storm cloud and swept across the ground. But this was open country, where it did no harm, we thought. Later, when we were traveling the north road, we saw the effects of the funnel, and I was shocked. The tornado had gone through an orchard without uprooting a tree, but had laid the entire orchard over almost parallel to the ground. It remained so in all the years that followed.

In the southern part of Nowata County another tornado swept along the side of the highway where it rolled up a fence neatly and firmly and left it there in a coil while the funnel whirled on to do other damage. A friend had a round corral full of cattle and the storm stood it up on its side like a wheel full of cows. Some of the cows did not make it. The same storm took the roof off his house, but left a rocking chair standing where it had been stored in the attic.

The effects of a tornado are bizarre indeed. Huge items are shredded like small bits of confetti and strewn across the land or high in treetops. Meanwhile a nearby house or car might be totally untouched.

An intelligent person does not "brave it out" when there is a storm in Oklahoma. The capricious behavior of a tornado is uncanny. The air crackles with ozone and the whole sky takes on an aura eerily threatening, like a panther crouched to spring.

And so, after that summer of dought, the rains came, brought by a big storm, just as Grandmother had predicted. When she saw it coming over the hills, Grandmother dashed for cover with me, my mother and the famous tin box in tow.

I was terrified of the black clouds billowing down upon us from the northwest, but I've never forgotten my mother's words. "Don't you know," she said calmly, "the Lord can take care of you."

WIND

WIND IS A SYMBOL of the Great Holy Spirit. It carries life, changes the seasons, lifts, opens, tests the durability and power of every living thing to survive. Clouds gather and disperse by its force and people smilingly predict what it will do. The smiles say plainly that this is a prediction by the best methods ever discovered — but only a prediction.

Wind is not comfortable, not to animal or to man. Though it blows away winter and brings moisture to feed the green fields, it also brings changes that are not so welcome. It lifts huge trees and buildings effortlessly and lays them on the earth again as though earth had spit them up. Great ships labor in wind-driven ocean waves and only grace brings them safely into harbor.

Wind is a natural force and a spiritual force at the same time. The breath of life flares the nostrils, fills the lungs — and gives flight to birds. So varied is its purpose that its tremendous power and immense gentleness are taken for granted, seldom recognized as gifts of grace.

Blessings that come without human labor are often overlooked. Grace does not require effort or purity or goodness, but comes on every puff of wind, to the person who is ready to receive.

THE FINE ART
OF WINE MAKING

SUMMER RAINS were unusually heavy one year and elderberry bushes were laden with huge clusters of dark purple berries. I wanted to eat the berries and asked permission. "Go ahead, " I was told, but when I did I found the elderberries, sour, unappetizing. E lis i did make jelly from them, but strawberry and blackberry jelly were so much better. The main use for elderberries was to make elderberry wine, an activity that was illegal in Oklahoma at that time. I didn't know anything about wine, but I was enchanted by the elderberries, so beautiful in their abundance.

One particular summer day E lis i came from the woods with a big basket of herbs and greens. She went into the shed, came out with a hammer, and started back to the woods. I wanted to follow her. If E lis i was going to kill a snake, I wanted to see it. But Mama shook her head and I had to go with her to sort and wash the greens.

An hour or so passed and then E lis i came out of the woods with a smile on her face. Aunt Nina was with her and they were laughing about something.

Supper time was one of my favorite times of the day. The whole family would gather and tell stories and laugh together. Mama said supper was the time when people should laugh. She said it was good for digestion. In our family it was not allowed to bring grievances to the table.

E lis i brought a huge black bread pan, scooped out hot biscuits and put them on everyone's plate. Other bowls were passed and the joking continued. Papa always offered to put sugar in the gravy to make it into pudding, and Uncle Carl said something colorful about what it would be. And then suddenly, Grandma asked, "Carl, did you see Sheriff Owen today?" She didn't say she had seen him but asked a simple question. Uncle Carl's jovial manner subsided and he soon left the table. After a time he slipped off into the woods. Everyone laughed but said nothing.

A few days passed before Mama told me that E lis i Grandma and Aunt Nina had found a wine press in the woods. They knew it belonged to Uncle Carl. They set the stage to make Uncle Carl think the sheriff had been around — but it was they who beat the wine press into pieces with their hammers. The incident was never again mentioned and even as I grew to adulthood, I never knew if Uncle Carl knew it was E lis i that put safeguards on his future.

A NEW
GRANDFATHER

AT THE END OF ONE SCHOOL DAY, my cousins and I got off the school bus and crossed the yard to our house. E lis i Grandma met us at the door and she was smiling and happy.

"Come on in, children, and meet your new grandfather."

Wide-eyed and wondering, we went in. An old, white-haired gentleman stood up and greeted us with smiling eyes. His ruddy complexion made him look like a congenial Santa Claus. It was some time before we learned he was stone deaf and had no idea what Grandma had said.

He wasn't really our new grandfather, just a poor old man, like many poor people in those depression days, wandering through the country without food or a place to sleep. This old gentleman was clean and appeared to be intelligent and Grandma asked him to stay for supper.

When Uncle Carl and Papa came in they met the guest. Grandma didn't use the "new grandfather" line on them, but they quickly caught on that the man was deaf. Uncle Carl loved the whole situation and told the old man some outlandish stories. The man would smile and nod his head as though he understood.

We all sat down to eat and Grandma brought a huge black pan of hot biscuits to the table and emptied it into a bowl. Then she set the hot pan on the wood box to cool. My cat, Jawbreaker, decided he would smell of the bread, but when he discovered the pan was hot he skittered sideways and knocked the bread pan to the floor.

Uncle Carl didn't miss a lick in telling his stories. He looked at my "new grandpa" and said, "We're afraid that cat will mess in the bread pan."

The old man smiled and agreed that it could happen — though he didn't know what Uncle Carl had said. Grandma told Uncle Carl to make a bed for him in the school bus that Papa had parked close to the house. It may not have been the warmest bed, but it was better than sleeping on the ground.

The old man must have left early the next morning because I never saw him again. The more I thought about him, the more I thought that he may have been deaf — and again, maybe not. Maybe his deafness was a ploy to get sympathy, food and a place to sleep. I always wondered. I had the feeling that he heard my grandmother tell us children he was our new grandfather, and probably he heard all of Uncle

Carl's fantastic tales, and he heard that we were afraid of what the cat would do in the bread pan.

If I was to have picked a new grandfather, this one would have been a good choice, for he was happy and pleasant to have around. But he didn't stay. It is strange how strongly I felt he heard and knew everything. We both loved his fooling the family and carrying it off with such aplomb.

MESSAGE
WITHIN A MESSAGE

AT THE TIME OF A FULL MOON, nature's music carries through the woods and over the hills. It has a quality all its own, and if we listen quietly but with an open spirit, the music opens a new ear. Wonderful things await us. A whippoorwill's plaintive call wavers through air currents and another whippoorwill answers. The sound stirs the heart and gives rise to emotions that open other doors to deeper understanding.

A coyote pup sets up an unbelievable wail that is soon joined by others. The sound is not so different from Indian voices in high worship or simply in high spirits. A time such as this brought what one American Indian called "spiritual messages through the bushes." He heard, and it was enough. He did not need a piece of paper or voice mail through a machine. This particular communication was closer to him than his own breath, closer yet than hands and feet. It was not diluted by those who have no understanding. He could discern the reality of it and he could rely on its integrity — and on his own capacity to receive what he heard.

Nothing sharpens the senses and stirs the spirit like standing quietly in the moonlight. We are transported back to ancient times and yet ahead to times we cannot fathom except by the Spirit. Never be caught in ignorance — listen and know what wonders are possible. Listen to the Voice and know you cannot completely plumb the depths of its glorious meaning but you can gradually hear and perceive your own profound blessings.

OLD WAH-YA´,
MY FRIEND

THE SOUL OF THE CHEROKEE is forever immutable in its love for a kindred spirit. And yet that love of brother is never so strong as the love for things of nature. So closely woven are these allies of spirit, we can sense that all things are brothers, all people are one with nature. All nature keeps a constant pace; it never forgets and never loses the love of life for which it was made.

I was very young when my soul first took flight. It was free with the freedom of the redbird vibrating its breast among the leaves of the dogwood.

The early morning sun had just begun to penetrate the thick dust on the road to the creek and my bare toes stung when I dug them in deep. It felt good at first, like something bitter tastes sweet until it gets farther back on the tongue. The air was hot, but my cotton dress and bloomers were airy and comfortable as I lightly skipped through sunlight rich with the fragrance of earth and the lush woods nearby. My feet never toughened to going barefoot in hot dust and I began to hippety hop on the sides of my heels. I headed for a spot of shade no larger than one of my feet. Poised like a bird with one foot drawn up, my eye measured the distance from where I stood to the thick shade of the woods ahead where the redbird's whistle beckoned me.

I raced across the hot ground to a wooden foot bridge spanning a large ravine leading to the creek. There I rested. I hung over the railing to watch the water. I watched a leaf float out of sight beneath the oak slabs, then I ran to the other side to watch it float into sight again. But a bluebird flitted by, turning my vision down the lane. If it had not caught my eye I may never have seen old Wah-ya' Smith as he disappeared down the slope to the creek. Old ones say he is called Wah-ya', or Wolf, because he raised a wolf from a pup to full grown and then set it free. His love of all wildlife was reflected in his almost turquoise-colored eyes, clear like fresh water, that belied his degree of Cherokee blood and tattled on our French neighbors to the north. His black hair, only slightly streaked with silver, was tied back with a leather thong, and his bright blue shirt deepened the brown of his lined face. His solemnity was only broken by the twinkling of his eyes — and one hour spent in his company, with or without words, was a serene experience.

Oblivious to spots of hot dust, I ran after him shouting, "Wait for me!"

It was my privilege to tag after him frequently while he pretended to fish, but he spent most of his time with a serious expression on his face while he sketched on a pad of paper he always carried with him. Sometimes he had a paint box and would let me have a little piece of paper to make colors on. Usually, he would let me doodle and mess up the paper until I tired of it. Today, out of frustration, he said, "Little one, I hate to have you grow up ignorant!" And he started then teaching me to see the shape and color and depth of my heritage — and to think about what I was seeing.

When I looked up at a tree he pointed to and said, "It's green," he cuffed me on my back with the flat of his hand and raised his voice.

"Now can't you see anything? That tree is not green — not just green! Look at it! See the trunk? See the bark? What color?"

"Gray."

He scowled, "You still don't know. The bark is gray and black and even white, according to how the light strikes it. See the crevices in the rough bark? Mostly black. But some of it is gray and where it is edged with light it is white."

At that moment, I felt the same presence that came to me when I did something less than admirable and my mother would ask, "What would your Aunt

Maria say if she knew you did that?" Aunt Maria was my grandfather's full-blood Cherokee sister and she had royal dignity one would expect of a lady educated in the Cherokee Female Seminary. I straightened my shoulders and silently gathered my spirit and turned it around in my mind. Suddenly, I could see what Wah-ya' was telling me. I clapped my hands together and laughed out loud!

I had never really forgotten those things. Like something preserved in amber, my age-old vision took its place. The rough bark of the old oak was truly beautiful!

"When you think you have learned all the lessons in life, Little One, look again. And remember a tree in early morning will have a different color, perhaps all shades of green from sunlight filtering the color through leaves. Past noon, when the light is gold and yellow, it would be still different. And what if it was raining? The blues and grays would settle in. Remember to look at things and consider where you are viewing them from. The time and place from which you judge life will make it look different from how you see it at other times — or how others may see it," he added quickly.

And then my companion pointed to a clump of violets blooming on the moist sod and asked, "What color?"

This time I took longer to answer, for my new eyes were seeing things I had not seen before. The violets were like something from a valentine, clustered in the center of waxy heart-shaped leaves. I peeked into the face of one tiny violet and found the deep center to be pale amethyst with deeper shades of purple, all colors of the evening sky as it reached the edge of each petal. Each flower was so perfect and dewy velvet that I almost forgot to answer him.

"Well?"

"The centers are almost white and then pink and purple."

"And the leaves?"

I carefully examined the tender stems that were ivory and pale green, and then deep, rich green, so dark it was almost black.

"Well! Maybe there's hope for you after all," Wah-ya' chuckled. "You can sit and be still so as not to scare away my fish, or you can get on home."

I knew he wanted more to be alone than to fish, and I had no desire not to be welcome again, so I left without a word. It seemed right with him as he only said what was necessary, and he could see I was leaving.

Leaving the cool creek bank did not lessen my curiosity. I was aware of the whole world that had always been and would go on being forever new. The road was beginning to cool as the rays of the afternoon sun touched only the tops of the trees and filtered here and there. I saw a sunspot on the water flowing under the bridge as I crossed back over and I stopped to watch it turn to pure molten gold. A pinch of dust I sprinkled through the sunlight floated and turned like thousands of sparkling glittering flecks of gold. A sudden gust of wind jarred a clump of oak leaves loose and it bounced off my foot. I picked up the acorns with the innate knowledge that one of them might be an oak tree — or have the potential to become one. With a stick I pushed back the rich black loam at the end of the bridge and planted the acorns, wondering which one would make a tree for the birds to sing in and the squirrels to climb.

I started to move on, but a rabbit, completely unaware of me, sat munching wild lettuce by the side of the road. His breast was the softest white fur and he had shades of gold and tan curving over his back, which was tagged with a white cotton tail. His pinkish ears lay flat to his back and his jaws wiggled as he nibbled. I was so intent on watching him that he gave me an awful start when he shot straight up in the air and gave a funny squeak! There was a whir of fur as one rabbit ran under another and each took his turn leaping straight up. I had never seen rabbits at play before and my first thought was to run tell Mama.

I suddenly realized I didn't have to tell anyone. Mama already knew because she was the one who had silently and serenely built this awareness into me, calling me to sit beside her to watch the sunset glowing rich and golden on the horizon. Or she would point out the evening star as it gleamed like a single jewel against dark blue velvet. I learned to watch the new moon from crescent to robust fullness. She helped me discover the morning star as the symbol of the One Spirit who created us with all goodness and provision.

Watching all this with my knees drawn up to my chin, I felt warm and comfortable. And when dawn broke over my world and the first rays of sunlight shot all colors of rose across the morning star, I felt a depth and peace that the years would not be able to scatter.

This new sensitivity to life was unlimited — only I could limit it by clouding my vision and sinking within. G go hi yo hga? Who are you looking for? I am looking for myself. I am always looking for my spirit to lead me onward and upward to new life and new awareness.

Just wait until I tell my friend Wah-ya'!

LEAVES FROM
A COON TREE

FOUR LITTLE INDIANS, little Cherokees, caught in a trap called a schoolroom.

Cousins, all within a year of the same age, all in the third grade of a small country school. Each of us had a special quality — at least, the way I told it. After our first day of school, Mama asked me who was the smartest among the four of us, and I told her, "Wennie." Then she asked, "Who can write the best?" I told her, "Breck."

Then she asked, "Who is the nicest?"

I told her Oren was the nicest — and when she asked me who was the best looking, I said, "I am."

None of us thrived on being penned up in a schoolroom. We had enjoyed a few years on sunny creek banks, listening to the wind in the trees and hearing the fish-bird calling to us, and it was hard to leave these things. But only Wennie took steps to avoid missing any part of it.

Wennie was oldest and he was our guardian angel. He was the one that cried when one of us got hurt. He was the spiritual big brother. We were proud of him because he could play hooky or "be sick," as it seemed his privilege to do, and still come to school on test day and make better grades than we did. Wennie obviously did not lack intelligence. His absences were what made our teacher write on his year-end report card that he would have to take the third grade over again.

But when school began the following autumn, Wennie went with us into the fourth grade. We asked him what he was doing there, and he told us, "I 'moted myself."

We approved of Wennie's decision, and no one else ever checked the records.

The four of us loved the woods, the creek, the great outdoors in all seasons. We knew the trees by heart, we hunted the skunks and possums. We ate the wild berries and paw-paws, and we spent hours "noodling" fish with our bare hands in the scattered pools left in summer's drying creek beds.

We were exceedingly shy, and it was devastating to be sent to the front of the class to work arithmetic on the blackboard. But Fridays were easier for us because it was the last school day of the week and we were usually in high spirits.

Some days were easier than others because of school assembly — a time when all the classes came together in the gymnasium to see the children from the oil fields tap-dance and play the piano. These assemblies were nothing like the stomp dances we were used to. There were no drums. The only boring part was when the superintendent kept droning on and on. We discovered if we sat back quietly and narrowed our eyes to slits, we could see a red aura around Mr. Schultz. Wennie said it was because he was hot. We agreed.

One particular Friday was best of all. It was toward the end of our fourth year and our teacher was filling the time with special projects. She told the class to bring a leaf from a favorite tree to show the class and tell about it. Now, this was something we knew about! The oil-field kids may have known arithmetic — but we knew our trees. The only hard part for us was choosing only one leaf from the variety we had grown up with and lived with and loved every day. It seemed almost disloyal to select one when so many were worthy of notice.

Even Wennie came to school on Monday with a leaf in his hand and primed to tell about it. The others — all beneath our status as tree experts — seemed to take forever to tell about silver maples, plum, apple. Then, came Wennie's turn.

He looked around to make sure we three were behind him all the way. He stood up, hitched up his overalls, and a lock of dark hair fell across his freckled nose as he shyly turned to show the class his leaf.

When the teacher prompted him to tell what kind of leaf it was, he said, "My leaf is from a coon tree."

She was not amused. After what seemed to be a very long time, she spoke sharply, "Wendell! There is no such thing as a coon tree."

We were stunned. Of course, there was! All eyes were on Wennie, but he stood his ground. If there was one thing he knew about it was coon trees.

"Yes, Ma'am, there is," he said. "There's a coon tree down by the old Casebeer house."

All three of us vigorously nodded our heads in agreement. But the other children looked at each other and covered their mouths to hide mischievous giggles. Even Miss Terrell started to laugh, but changed her mind. She said, "Go ahead, Wendell, tell us about it."

Wennie was shaken for a minute. He had been so well prepared — and then to have his leaf denied and laughed at — now he was rattled. But he had a wealth of knowledge about coon trees. He looked first at us, and then, with his eyes straight ahead, he began.

"Well, a coon tree can be any kind of tree in the woods. It can be a walnut or a pecan or even a big ole oak. But it has to be big, and it has to have a hole away up high . . . because, you see, that's what makes it safe for the mama coon to raise her babies there. The hole is really a scar from some time when the tree was hurt and the wind and rain and hot sun kept it from being like other trees. When it hollowed out, a mama coon picked it to build her nest, and that tree never could go back and be just an ordinary tree."

And he sat down.

The look of amusement was gone from our teacher's face. Wennie had not just told us about one tree, but about something wounded being elevated to a special status. She went on to tell us in our language that regardless of what happens to us we can turn it to an advantage — that sometimes a trauma can be a turning point toward helping others in a way we might never have dreamed — like Wennie's coon tree.

Show and tell continued, but Wennie was the star. And he still is to this day. Except now he shines from heaven — and we see him with God in the clouds and we hear him in the wind.

PLAN FOR GOOD. Give yourself something to look forward to and it will motivate you. When our enthusiasm lags, energy vanishes for lack of nourishment. We do not always have a natural flow of energy because too much happens to keep us anxious. Adrenaline can rush through our veins so that we have only nervous energy — or else we fall asleep.

Don't let anyone convince you to accept something because they have accepted it. If you have a flicker of hope, a remnant of faith, it can outgrow your present problem and give you new insight on how not to be a victim of hopelessness. Rise up and make your own decisions. Open your mind and spirit to new understanding and new ability to overcome any problem — especially inertia.

What appears to be impossible may be the wall you can only see from your present stance. If you are willing to give thanks for something you want before you see it, you will not be disappointed. Be constant and faithful to your goals, show gratitude — and one day you will look back and wonder why you ever doubted.

Quanah Parker was taking his small Comanche son on his first hunting trip, and all the way the boy said, "But Father, I do not have a bow."

Parker said wisely, "Son, you have lots to learn before you notch a bow."

And so it is with each of us — but we have to take our first steps.

AS A CHILD OF SPIRITUAL NATURE, I had the freedom of the land and woods, and I wandered with contented pleasure among the trees and wild plants and waded in the shallow streams. I learned to sit quietly, not even moving an eyelid so that I could watch the squirrels chatting with each other and see the rabbits at play.

The woods and all its contents became a part of me, a beloved communion so that I was able to perceive things that others did not know. Reason and logic did not seem to be a part of what I learned; the lessons were spiritual. I learned not to bring thought in from outside but to stand quietly to receive what I was supposed to know.

All the parts of woods were not to my liking, for I knew in my heart that certain areas were off-limits. When I reached the edge of these places, a darkness lay over me and I backed away like a bird avoiding a trap.

For this very reason, I had no fear the day I was walking beneath the trees and I came on a figure knelt in prayer. It was a man whose age was not important but he was in a trance-like position and he did not move the whole time I sat by him. His right hand covered his eyes beneath the brim of his hat, and the coarse fabric of his long coat covered most of his feet and legs.

After a brief time I heard him whisper and it was not a language I had ever heard. It made no sense to me as it went on for a few minutes. I could see that he was totally unaware of my presence. Quietly I got up and left. I went along home and told my mother, "There was a man in the woods praying and it was not in any language we speak." She seemed to know what it was, though she did not know who it was. When I pressed her to tell me, she said, "It is not our people's way. The man has a gift of tongues, his own prayer language that no one else can understand unless it is revealed."

Our people do not do it this way? I often wondered. Perhaps some did not tell, the way I did not tell what came to me. Throughout all the years I have wondered about the man and what he prayed. Was he in agony or ecstasy? Did he receive an answer to his prayer, or was he simply praising and giving thanks? Did he know I was there or how he affected me for all this time?

Not our people's way? Grandfather Sequichie was a minister who spoke to Cherokees in their own language. It seemed strange to me that, since he was the good man that he was, God did not tell him how to pray in his own special prayer language.

Somehow, I can look through a window into a peaceful place, a place where the body and mind can rest and grow strong again. Can this be where the praying man was when I waited for him to do something? It must have been wonderful for the spirit to enter into this place and leave the body kneeling by a clump of trees.

There must be many wonderful things that I do not know. I will be watchful, I will listen — and I will see beyond my natural ability.

A SUDDEN BURST
OF SONG

SOMETIMES EVEN NATURE has difficulty sleeping on those nights when there is a sudden burst of music from the mockingbird as though it could no longer contain its song.

The song of the night bird is a serenade to life, a tension reliever for deeper inner relaxation. It brings with it an awareness that life is good.

When there is such awareness there is much less need to constantly worry about the trials that come with daylight. We learn to take our ease when we can. Then we are grateful for a time of sleep, a chance to rest.

It may be that nature's music was important to us when I was growing up because we had no musical instruments at home or in the church. We sang together. There was an awareness of voices and the parts that made the singing music or strident noise. Nature's songs are never hard on the ears. Singing with Mama was pleasant because her voice was soft and gave harmony to most any song. Driving at night with Papa was a favorite time because we always harmonized singing "Precious Memories."

During an anthrax outbreak, Uncle Carl had the unpleasant job of burning the carcasses of whiteface cattle to stop the disease from spreading. We rode horseback many miles back in hilly ranch pastures hunting for cows separated from the herd. Uncle Carl would be riding ahead and I would be trailing along on Figger, but I could hear his Indian voice singing "The Cattle Call" and I loved it though I hated the disease we were fighting.

Now, when I am standing in moonlight and I hear the midnight minstrel serving up his overflow of day-time songs, I am brought again to the memory of these precious voices singing — and once again time takes me back and I recognize special qualities of each one. They are telling me they still sing with me.

And when I hear Cherokees sing "Amazing Grace" in their beautiful language, my heart is with the ancients once more.

E LIS I'S
PASSING

WHEN I WAS TEN YEARS OLD, E LIS I DIED. I never knew what ailed my grandmother. She always appeared frail and I never thought much about it. All I knew was that my dear grandmother, who was my friend and walking companion, left me suddenly, and I rebelled. I decided that I was not going to bear this in a normal way, that I would be sick as well. Even then I knew the power of spoken words and I used it.

Soon after E lis i's death I heard Mama crying. She had handled the situation with composure until she went into the garden E lis i had tended so lovingly and saw there on the path, my grandmother's footprint. I couldn't stand for my mother to cry. I grew more and more silent and refused to eat.

Mama came to me and put her arm around me and asked if I was feeling well. I told her I did not feel well at all. I remember she lifted my hair and looked at my neck and down my collar. Then she said to Aunt Nina and Aunt Alma, "She has the measles."

E lis i had always kept me at home as much as she could to keep me from contracting childhood diseases.

If she was not going to stay around and protect me, I thought defiantly, I would have them all. I broke out with a million red bumps.

I will never forget the day the hearse came into our driveway and I knew it was time to tell E lis i goodbye. In those times, people usually had the casket brought in the house, but our house was too small for all those people, so Mama put her arm around me and took me out to the hearse where they opened the casket and let us view my beloved grandmother. She looked beautiful and at peace. Her snow white hair was combed softly back and she had on a lilac dress. Her hands had no garden dirt on them. Instead her nails were perfectly manicured. I thought, "Well, if I have to live with this, I can." And as Mama walked me back into the house someone put a dish of pork and beans in my hands. I had never eaten pork and beans before. Suddenly, for the first time since E lis i died, I was hungry and I ate.

Even though I was covered with measles, nothing could keep me from attending E lis i's service. On a beautiful sunshiny day over two hundred people gathered at the church, a tiny white building which couldn't possibly hold all those people. They set up seats and a pulpit in the churchyard and held the service outdoors. When I saw all the beautiful flowers I had a private laugh with E lis i. She had told me many times that if anyone ever put an artificial flower on her grave she would kick it off. I remember saying silently, "Rest yourself, Grandma, these flowers are real."

Many years have gone by, but the garden where Grandma had left her footprint is still there — a garden that was once full of hollyhocks and roses and even violets beneath the plum trees. Today I have only to go on our Indian land and I feel her presence. Here, I know that she still loves me and she knows I love her dearly. For this reason, I have never been able to sell the land. Many offers have been made and potential buyers have asked my friends why "that Indian woman" will not sell.

The barn is gone, but I still smell the hay and hear the stamping feet of the cows waiting to be milked. The east hill still brings up the sun and persimmon trees still grow where the old shed once stood. Bricks from the foundation of the house are still on my hearth. I only have to touch them to see a lifetime unfold. Special people, special little secret places come to mind and my heart overflows with gratitude that I grew up among these hills. If love was tangible and could be seen, these acres would be overflowing.

Because of some similar "Indian" notion, no doubt, several years after we all moved away, Papa went out to the old house that was slowly crumbling and burned it to the ground. I never asked him why he had to do that, though today I would love to have one little board out of that house. But you don't question an old Indian when he has his secret reasons. I should know.

OLD-TIMER

I WATCHED THE OLD-TIMER come toward me on bent and wiry legs. He slowly lowered himself to a wooden bench as though his knees might suddenly give way. We sat in the sunlight of a warm spring day and I waited for him to break the silence.

He was an old man who had spent many years in law enforcement. Today he would speak about his life. He had known all kinds of people, the best and the worst.

"When I sit quietly — as I so often do these days — I look back and remember folks from my past. Though some of them were scoundrels, I have come to miss them, come to appreciate the part they played in my life. Perhaps everything would have been less colorful without them — and I can think of no other reason for finding anything of value to recall. Most of them were what they were, no frills, no lies, no pretense. They hid behind nothing, felt no remorse, and went on their merry way — often leaving devastation behind them.

"I ask myself, what of these persons? Did we earn them by the choices we made — or is it possible that much of the world's goings-on simply crash our gates and slip in unnoticed until we begin to smell the sour odor of rotten apples?

"But looking back over a gallery of almost forgotten faces, I hated only a few — and learned to give that up as well. I discovered they were not worth my time, not a tenth of one percent of my peace. Yes, they robbed and stole and plundered, and they killed. But now most of them are dead. Few ever asked forgiveness. Did they assume they had it? Or did they recognize the fact that they ravaged honor and left peace in shreds?

"When these people met their God, and all of us do, were they forgiven before they took that final step? Did God meet them in a secret passageway and say, 'This is your last chance.' Or, did they hope to break down the doors of heaven the way they broke those on earth?

"Maybe I am pondering these things because I am very old, and I will one day soon find myself in that passageway. It awes my deepest feelings, but it does not frighten me. I have forgiven — and much to my amazement I have forgotten as well. When I was much younger, I would meet someone that had mistreated me as a youth, and they would rush to me and shake my hand and ask about my well-being. I would wonder in some dismay if they had forgotten what they had done. I wondered if they had found deeper meaning, and then I asked myself if they simply didn't care. I found myself skirting around them for fear I would show my distaste. But then came the pity. They seemed to be clutching at straws of once-upon-a-time. The need to recapture something of the past made them my friend.

"Now, I am that friend. Now, I have lived long enough to know what is important. My child, it is love. I have come to love the unlovely. What greater gift than to lay down the past and sit here in peace enjoying every minute as I once did. If this is a closing cycle, let it be. Another far greater opens for me when I decide it is the time."

When that time came, I doubt he had regrets — at least not many. Honors to his memory go on, and the time will come when we can again sing "Precious Memories" together the way we used to sing it, in harmony.

SAYING AHEAD
OF TIME

EVEN AS A CHILD I knew the power of the spoken word, for it seemed that I could say what would happen ahead of time. This trait often took my mother by surprise. I would be feeling joyful, elated, and tell her it was because we were going to get ice cream that day. Not wanting me to be disappointed, she would settle me down with quiet denials. But invariably my prediction would prove to be true. Later that day my Aunt Alma would unexpectedly drive into our driveway and ask if we wanted to ride into town to get ice cream.

One time I told Mama that our sow, "that old pretty pig" was going to have babies. Mama assured me that was not true. A few days later I found the sow in the cake house with a new litter of piglets. I still remember Mama's surprise when I rushed to the house and told her there were twelve "cold-white" baby pigs. "What are you talking about?" she asked. "Coal is black."

"But the baby pigs are white, Mama," I assured her. "Cold white!" And I took my disbelieving mother out to the cake house to show her the newborn piglets, white as snow.

LISTEN AND HEED
THE LAWS

LISTENING IS ESSENTIAL. We cannot function well in anything if we cannot listen and hear. Listening with the mind and with the spirit can quicken us to wise decision-making and to understanding what others are saying to us that will help us make these wise decisions.

Chief Joseph of the Nez Perce wrote, "Our fathers gave us many laws, which they had learned from their fathers. These laws were very good." But if they are to serve us well, we must listen and heed. Because we listen and know does not mean we do what they tell us to do.

American Indians relied on hearing and remembering so that they could pass along information to those who followed. History was carried along in stories and teachings from generation to generation — a record of learning that gathered the wisdom and understanding of the ancients. Life was more beautiful, more peaceful, to those who lived according to the laws.

Life still rewards all who heed them. We are still able to use these ancient treasures if we will only do it.

WHAT EDEN WAS,
WHAT PARADISE
MAY BE

I PLANTED BEANS THIS MORNING. Standing in the fields, I surveyed the timberline and watched the egrets rise and settle again near the cattle. One of them hitched a ride on the back of a cow to catch the insects that swarm in the warm spring air.

Above me, the clear blue sky seems to be open to anyone who wants to rise into it. At one time that particular thought would have been preposterous, but now flying is an everyday occurrence. Who can say what powers we have. After all, the beans I dropped into musty turned-up soil will, within hours, take a new shape, and from the center of each one a green pointed sprout will emerge and burst the bean wide open.

Who would have known such power and energy was in the bean — the very essence of creation set in motion all those centuries ago. The sprout thrusts through the ground with greed for the sun, having been drawn up toward the very nourishment it needs. But even then, its shape is different. It is no longer a tender green sprout, but a thin, reedy stem from which green leaves will soon take shape. As time goes by, cream-white blossoms pop open and the centers are like tiny folded gloves. It is from this that a pod takes shape. With the pod come the multiple offspring of one tiny bean that was dropped into the earth.

We never know when we plant what size the harvest will be. If conditions are right, our harvest should be full and rich. But the first step is to plant good seed. It is not how much we plant, but the quality of what we plant that makes the difference.

I have learned that it is the same in giving to others as in planting a garden — we get a better crop if we give from the best we have.

So I have planted the best seed I could afford, and having covered them with my hoe, it comes to me that I am going to harvest as well. It is my responsibility to plant — but an even greater one to go back and harvest. I cannot do one thing without bearing the responsibility of it all. The price is believing in the good seed, but the labor is love — for the rewards are not just in planting but also in being able to stand here in the row and be a part of the nature of things. With the sun on my shoulders, I blend with nature and I am the highest form of creation, the best seed.

Could this be what Eden was — what Paradise may be?

BROTHER AND
SISTER HARRELL

THE CHURCH SERVICE had been completed and we were all in the cemetery, gathered around for the last prayer.

During the lull between getting everyone in place and Brother Harrell composing himself to begin the prayer, a skinny, snaggle-toothed character stood directly across the open grave from the family. Grinning widely, his alcohol-blurred eyes scanned the crowd until they focused on the preacher. His high-pitched voice crackled to break the silence.

"Brother Harrell," he started, "it's such a purty day, it's a damn shame we ain't got another one out here we could bury, ain't it?"

There was authority in the preacher's booming voice when he shouted, "Harry, we are going to have another one if you don't get yourself out of here."

If Brother Harrell did not leave me with the memory of great sermon, he and his tiny wife impressed me with their thrift. They lived in a tiny house with no bathroom. That was not out of the ordinary for those days. But the walls of the house and the out-house were artfully papered with clean newspapers. The bulky newsprint made good, cheap insulation. Both places were immaculate and hugely entertaining for those prone to tarry.

Beyond that, visiting the Harrells meant no joyful outbursts of laughter, no skipping, and no singing or whistling. And when they visited us, we suffered through a long strained hour of modest behavior, pious expressions, and critical looks at our bare feet and legs.

But Sister Harrell took her religion quite seriously. One time she read about the golden calf in the Bible and proceeded to beat her wedding ring to pieces on a rock.

On the other hand, I have heard of others doing the same thing without having read the Scriptures.

IT SEEMS ONLY YESTERDAY when the first cold wind blew in and laid flat the wild rose and turned it gray. Leaves changed colors and dropped. Snows fell and drifted. Winter raged and threatened to last forever. It did not. It only made us believe we would be eternally locked in a deep freeze. But its fury was spent even before it had used its allotted time.

A field that lay tranquil and still during winter's rampage drank the spring rain, responded to warm fingers of sunlight, and flowers edged in overnight.

Even before the snows were gone, the rolling hills took on a haze of green. The limbs of the willows around the pond turned pink as life rose in each branch. The first blooms, pink-and-white striped dayflowers, fragile lilies, and tiny three-petal blue-eyes carpet the edges of the meadow path, until it is impossible to step without pressing them down. But they bloom only briefly.

We have that same irrepressible quality of life, if we only knew it. We are the seeds that can throw off the pall of cold that threatens. The same energy, the same deep-seated urge to grow, lies within us and thrives at the touch of warmth. But when it seems that no one loves us, where do we get the warmth that helps us overcome repression? We get it from the Original Source that has an immeasurable stream of life-giving love.

It is strange that love is often thought to be a force outside ourselves. From our first breath we beg to be held, to be loved, to be cherished. If we are not shown the deep love we so need, it is not because we are unlovable but only that those we look to do not know how to give it. The human spirit, like a fragile flower crushed beneath stampeding herds, can be broken, bent, and nearly destroyed. But we have roots that go deeper than mere humanity. Our spirits have origins that no other person can touch, taint, or take from us. When we speak from that place at our roots, we speak with authority. I am well. I am free. I am what I claim to be.

When we begin to use the power of our tongues to renew and restore, we can no longer use it to destroy. What we say is our most creative work.

When we are flowers with damaged stems, we can wind ourselves around a life-giving support. However much we want to say that life is not worth it, remember the wild rose that has thousands of needle-sharp thorns. Think how it blooms. It is not coarse and straggly, but puts forth delicate pink clusters in profusion over the thorns.

In many unseen ways we are even more hardy than the wild rose. We can think. We can speak and believe. We can change our way of thinking and being. We can take this inner-child of ourselves in our arms and rock it and croon to it and tell it how much we love it. We just didn't know where He put our help. It was in us all the time, deep and beautiful and healing. This inner-love is the magnet that draws love from outside forces. This love cannot destroy but only enhances body, soul, and spirit. It was meant to do this.

FREE...
BUT NOT EASY

AS A CHILD, I WAS A FREE SPIRIT — whether my mother was aware of it or not.

I suspect that she knew. She had a way about her that enabled her to tune in to what was happening, even when no words were spoken. Mama ruled; I never doubted it. Once something went past my skin going inward, however, I ruled.

No one could tell what I was thinking — in fact, no one seemed to care as long as I was obedient. I wasn't always. My mind would drift and when I was told to come home, I might start in that direction, but stop to climb a tree, to sit and think with my nose pressed to my scruffy knees contemplating their musty odor.

Sometimes a rabbit or two would be playing beneath the tree, showing joy, leaping and chasing one another in circles. Why couldn't people do that, I wondered. What happened to our joy? When I was in the woods, I felt the Presence of the Spirit and I was joyous. But when I went to church with my mother, joy was not there.

I looked for it, waited for it. Sometimes I felt laughter as I sat with my cousins like stone children on a hard pew. Our laughter started when a man with palsy sat behind us and braced himself by holding onto our pew to control his shaking. At regular intervals, our pew shook violently, and with nothing else to entertain us, we looked at each other and the laughter was uncontrollable — until my mother and her sisters turned around, slapped our legs and frowned.

Frowning seemed to be a church-born habit. When people in church prayed they frowned as though they believed God would not listen and definitely would not answer. They talked a lot about who was dying and they preached too loud.

I learned to fear in church. I didn't learn to fear God; He was my Friend from the woods. But I learned to fear all the things that threatened us in church.

The only time I heard the preachers and congregation laugh was when someone put a button in the collection plate. One of the more expressive preachers, a fellow with ears like a Model-A coming down the road with both doors open according to Uncle Carl, said when he saw the button, "Well, preachers need buttons on their pants."

There was one lady preacher, with red hair and a ruddy complexion that reddened to scarlet when the man made the remark about the button, because everyone turned to look at her. I figured it served her right for saying all the children in the church were carnal creatures. I didn't know what carnal meant, but I knew if she said it about us, it couldn't be good.

Sitting in church was never easy for a free-spirited Cherokee girl used to worshipping outdoors where she could feel the presence of the Great Holy Spirit all around her.

WHERE IS THE SNOW that lay over these fields in winter? Where is the vapor trail once drawn through the morning sunrise? What happened to the tracks left by a mountain lion on the soft edges of the pond? Where are the snails that made silver lines across the garden walk? We see them, and then we do not see them. Once visible, but no longer there. Tracks! How can we believe in these things if we have no tangible evidence?

The snows have found the river and flowed on down to the sea. Vapor trails have all drifted into other air currents and slowly dissipated. The tracks of the mountain lion have melted into the silt of spring rains, and the silver paths of snails have been trampled away. Does nothing stay to prove it existed?

As faith wanes, new evidence appears. It comes in unlikely ways and in the most unlikely places. Who could have believed an unknown person left tracks — only a few in the beginning, but with time, so very many. An acre, or even more, covered with lilies, stretched through the woods like a remnant of bright orange fabric.

Blooms, thousands of them in muted oranges and yellows, dipped and nodded in the woodsy breeze, beckoning a believer to new evidence that long ago someone lived in these supposedly virgin woods. A few bulbs naturalized into thousands, creating breathtaking tracks — fresh evidence that renews a rare and exquisite miracle with every spring season.

New feet, new wheels, new tracks. Over and over we erase those that have gone before us. The evidence that remains is sometimes startling — as startling as the discovery of surreal blue eyes in the solemn face of my full-blood Navajo friend. It may have been the blue turquoise on his hatband that brought out the vivid blue of his eyes.

"Why, Mr. Hubbard, where did you get those blue eyes?"

His eyes crinkled at the corners, and for a moment, merriment danced across his bronzed face in a rare smile.

"My child, don't you know? We have traveled the world over!"

He had never been more than a few miles from his reservation, but his ancient ancestors had traveled far and wide. Tracks!

Wise King Solomon sang of such phenomena, "There be three things which are too wonderful for me, yea, four which I know not.

The way of an eagle in the air;
The way of a serpent upon a rock;
The way of a ship in the midst of the sea; and
The way of a man with a maid."
No tracks. There and gone.

We deny what we do not want to see, but sometime, somewhere, something always surfaces to prove it did exist.

Are we so depleted in our believing that we must have constant evidence? Only nothing leaves nothing. Or can we be open to new reason to believe every day — believe we will have what we need?

Will we ever be filled and satisfied with all we know? No. But we will always have unlimited spirits that go on living and asking, in this realm or in another much grander.

PRAIRIE
INDIAN

THOUGH MY ANCESTORS came from the southeastern woodlands, deep in my spirit, I have always known I was a prairie Indian. I want to know where I came from and I want to see where I am going. I can do that on this bald prairie where I first saw the light of day.

I spent endless hours of solitude riding Figger across a wide expanse of prairie, with nothing to break the view but grassy peaks that rose out of the ground to tremendous heights. My inner space is so akin to this land that rolls and softens in the sunlight, that I am sad when city cousins look on it with alarm.

"How empty!" they say.

It cannot be empty! It is open, but never empty. From the land itself to the limitless sky, it is all things most yielding. Sunlight warms and nourishes every living thing so that even the tiniest flowers are not overwhelmed by the space they have to cover. Cattle feed on tall grasses that turn rose-beige in winter and spring up lush and green in spring. Drifts of wildflowers, daisies and bright coreopsis compete with vivid Indian blanket and plumes of Indian-red paintbrush.

Warm rains sweep across in summer, stealing power from angry thunderstorms that rumble and threaten on the distant horizon. Tornadoes like whirling dervishes dip down in an angry yellow-green swirl, only to bounce harmlessly across the terrain and then telescope back up to the mother cloud.

Meadowlarks sing of summer skies and sunsets spread their glorious colors from some inexhaustible pallet, with nothing to hold them back but a few grazing horses silhouetted against the golden glow.

With evening, the only sound is the tremulous cry of the screech owl from its nesting place in the cleft of a limestone. Figger snuffles as he stops to strip away blades of prairie grass that squeak between his teeth.

As the last rays of sunlight slip behind the dark horizon, fireflies begin to flicker and dance. Grandmother always said the lightning bugs dance high when the weather is clear, and cling to the lower air currents when a change is due.

With nightfall, Venus is bold and vivid in the still-bright sky. Then, gradually, a hush falls over the land and the sky is one great, glittering canopy. Out of nowhere a meteor streaks across the horizon, dragging its orange tail — as if to say, this, too, will change.

In winter, snowfall envelops me in yet another world. Great flakes, like goose down from a feather bed, drift slowly down until there is no north, no south, no heaven or earth. Everything is suspended in space, a white world of no shape — and nothing to catch the softness but clumps of grasses and an occasional slab of limestone.

Slowly, the prairie becomes a great sheet of white paper, unmarked and waiting for me to write with my spirit. As I blend with this white world, a new existence rises in my consciousness — and I am more than I was. It is a world without complications, a space to wander in peace. It is a place kept in my inner space, a place of joy and praise to the Great Holy Spirit.

ROUNDING UP
THE CATTLE

IN RECENT YEARS, I opened Grandma's tin matchbox that held all the family deeds and papers. Among the things in the box were little black books my grandfather used to keep the hours for his teams of horses and himself when he built roads, bridges and culverts for the county.

I found papers from the bank where Mama had mortgaged two of her cows to borrow thirteen dollars to buy two more cows to increase the herd. It brought back memories of the many hours I spent as a girl on Figger's back herding those cows to drink in Big Creek and to graze in open fields.

Figger was originally a cutting horse — which means he was trained to go into a herd to bring out a certain cow or calf. He was very quick to move and to change directions with only a little pressure from knees on his sides. The only problem was, I didn't always intend to have him dart and swerve, and when he did it unexpectedly he threw me off.

This was what happened when I was rounding up cattle one day after a hot sticky shower had come through, watering nothing and making the summer heat worse. The cattle tried to cross the creek to the cornfield, Figger swerved to head them off, and I was thrown into a mass of cockleburs. Furious, scores of burrs tangling my long hair and caught in my clothes, I picked myself back up and remounted the horse. Then, I was required to swim Figger across the creek, under brush and small trees, to gather the stray cows back to the herd. Branches and leaves, still wet with rain slapped my face and arms as we struggled through the tangle of foliage. I was hot and wet and mad. Then, even worse, as we climbed up out of the creek I discovered a green snake between my hand and the reins. No matter how hard I try to forget, I still remember how that snake felt, wriggling against my arm. I dropped it and kicked Figger to jump into the creek again.

In a whirl of angry frustration I rounded up the cows and herded them back home to the pasture — a pasture with a little pond that was mostly sticky mud.

Mama didn't even scold me for carelessness when I went to her to get all the cockleburs out of my long hair. Of course, I didn't tell her about the wicked names I'd called those cows out there in the fields. Frankly, I don't think she would have blamed me.

OLD MAJOR

IN THE SPRINGS OF MY CHILDHOOD, I watched prairie fires lap across the land in red waves, and saw long rangy cowboys at the leading edge, with their wet gunnysacks slashing at the hottest part. Their faces were covered with soot, and ash perched on the tip ends of their hair jutting from beneath the rolled brims of their hats. Every wrinkle in their faces and every crease in their clothing collected soot and bits of burned grass and ash.

I recall Old Major, his limp chambray shirt soaked with sweat and coated with soot and ashes. He was once a big man, but years of cowboying and riding gave him a bent look that so often happens to men who spend their lives hunched forward in all kinds of weather. I have seen his sheepskin collar heavy with snow. I have seen his face sunburned and ruddy from many winds. But most of all, I remember his kindness with animals and humans, as well.

Old Major was always prepared for any kind of weather, had spent years anticipating what would be required of him. When a person is ready, Old Major said, much of the work is done. It follows a pattern that affords few surprises and little anxiety.

Old Major had dealt with cattle in his extreme youth, then with men in uniform, and then again with the herds, which had always been his first love. He would ride among the restless herd and sing in his soft tenor until they settled down like kittens in a basket. He kept an eye out for a sore foot, a small calf, or a weary cowboy.

They were all weary at the end of the day — but then most had not weathered the strain as well as Old Major. Most of them traveled with tense and edgy minds and bodies.

Old Major checked the singers and harmonica players before he hired them on as closely as he checked the ability of a cowboy. He knew at the end of the day there had to be a time of rest and relaxation. A new day required refreshed and rested men and animals to meet it.

I learned from Old Major — not just about riding the range and about prairie fires, but also about surviving life itself. I learned that it pays to be happy in spirit. I was always at his heels, and just knowing a bit of his wisdom has spared me many mistakes.

I know he never expected it, but I wonder if anyone ever thanked Old Major for what he had been to us.

WHISPER
OF THE LAND

ON THE DARKEST DAY IN WINTER, color is all around us — colors we do not expect to see, so we do not see them. They float in the early morning clouds that lie along the southeastern horizon, and hover in the crevices of the hills at midday. In evening, the western horizon is moving, breathing rose-gold and purple — all shades of purple.

The truth is that we are not tuned to the joy of color the way we are to dreary things. If our minds are caught on dismal colorless thoughts, our eyes have little chance of seeing beyond them.

To overcome my own color blindness, I have spent long hours in the orchard and surrounding areas. Here I find the solitude I need to study the life and color of the land. I have trudged over this ground when it was frozen solid, when it wept with too much rain, when it was dry and dusty, and when it was verdant with growing plants and trees and wild flowers.

I shared everything I saw and comprehended with my notebook, kept minute details about everything I observed. I learned never to assume a thing. I could never rely on memory to recall exactly how a wild strawberry looked, and I knew it would look different when a week had passed.

Every day and every walk was different. The incredible things happening were too important not to keep a record — how a meadow was ablaze with dew gems, the roundness of a deer's rump as it scampered across the field, and how the smoke from a farmer's brush pile spiraled like a blue corkscrew into the atmosphere.

Everything is full of life for such a short time. The image must be as important in my notebook when I read it again as it was when it happened. It must be able to live again on the page in another season.

My winter notebooks go with me into spring, and my spring notes are soon filled out with summer pictures. I record and record, because each image must have time to work through my own fingers and my own consciousness to live on paper.

The word is only a part of the spirit, but it feeds the one who cannot stop to see, to experience the purples of the land. I cannot assume readers will know what I have seen, how a flower blooms, how a bird flies, or what fragrance is. To trigger someone else's imagination to see for themselves, is to come full circle to reawaken my own.

Sometimes when the snow is flying and juncos feed at my window, I close my eyes and see the lush violets that bloom along the banks of the river in another season. I can see the moss-green leaves fat with sap, and lined with crisp white veins to support the weight. The leaves are centered with lilac and purple blooms that are so velvety they hold every drop of dew that falls upon them.

No one should miss the purples that accent nature. We who record the whisper of the land must live in it, breathe it, and bring it forward.

Wonders await us all. But our spirits must be kindled to see and to feel. Then, when we are weary, when all the color has drained from our spirits, we can tap into the life of the land again and find a healing peace.

SEB AND ME,
AND FUN

SOMETIMES, when I get tired while writing, I just relax and let my imagination go where it will. At such times, things come through that I never expect, voices not mine, with words not of my making. One such voice is that of Seb.

Seb came to me when I was struggling to put my own memories into words, and he introduced himself like this:

"Once a very long time ago, me lived. T'is not an easy one, but t'is not a bad one. T'is a necessary one.

"I live the day and sleep the night and feel hunger and feel good when eat.

"No time is lost and no time gained. We live in view of the mountain with sun. It says morning and it says evening. We talk when we need. We stay silent most. No one sick, no one tired, no one worry.

"Seb find rock. Pink with gold. Eyes shine. No one know. Looks pretty. We like. We hunt more. Find more, share. Find more. We no share. I take. He take. I shove. He shove. I go west. He go east. Lonely. Rocks throw down. I go east. He come west. Meet. No more hunt rock.

"Toe hit rock. Rock blue. Blue and gold. He see. We hunt more. Find many. Share? All in pile. Not work. Mine his, his mine. Not work. I give mine him. He give his me. We take to cave. Build wall of pretty rock. Sit down and like.

"Sun on mountain say morning. Sun no on mountain say night."

I'm always happy when Seb comes to speak. It eases my heart to know that writing isn't drudgery. I have learned the wisdom of play: When you get tired, go another direction.

THE SHERIFF'S
OFFICE

DURING HIS YEARS AS SHERIFF of Nowata County, Papa was always on duty, always ready to deal with whatever came his way, even though things did get a little rambunctious at times.

Anytime he had to go back in the cell block, he would take off his revolver and prepare himself to mix with the prisoners. A couple of them were aware of this and decided the next time he came in they would lock him up and escape. They did exactly as they planned except the old Indian was more of a fighter than they thought and they did not get the chance to lock him in. They rushed out the door and one of them got into his car which was curbside while the other ran around the courthouse and disappeared. The sheriff leveled the sights of his revolver on the windshield of the car and was prepared to fire when the man jumped out and held up his hands in surrender. As he escorted the prisoner back to jail, someone asked him what he planned to do about the escapee.

"Oh, I'll go down to his mother's and arrest him," the sheriff said calmly. Then he added, "They always go to their mother's and get into bed." He was exactly right. Both men went to prison with extended terms.

Another time, men playing dominoes in a nearby room heard the telephone ring in the sheriff's office, and heard the sheriff answer.

"Yes, I probably know who she is," he told somebody on the line.

The call was from a little town to the north and the hotel keeper was telling the sheriff to come and get a woman who was drunk and shooting firecrackers in her room. When he arrived, he discovered she had been entertaining gentlemen friends as well. So he took advantage of that mind-set and told her to go with him to town. She was delighted, until he pulled up to the curb in front of the courthouse. When she saw he'd tricked her, she began kicking and called him every name in the book. Finally, he managed to catch one of her legs and drag her up the sidewalk, through the sheriff's office and into a cell. It was an arrest that the courthouse domino players would talk about for years to come.

Then there was the time the local grocer called to say he had a man in his store with thirty dozen fresh eggs in a suitcase — and, oddly enough, he didn't think the man was sane. The man was brought in to the sheriff's and, to no one's surprise, was deemed unsafe to be on his own. He was put in a cell until a doctor could see him, but he spent his time lapping his thumb and pressing on the brads in the cell in an effort to electrocute the sheriff. Over and over he tried to get results but nothing happened. He would say, "Wait a minute, Sheriff," and the sheriff would stand patiently for his execution. The man would lap his thumb or finger and push on a brad and ask, "Did I get you that time?"

Over the next few days the prisoners feasted on the thirty dozen eggs — boiled, fried, however they wanted them fixed.

During the man's stay in the jail, the county clerk who was a compassionate little man, came down to reason with the patient. He walked into the cell block and approached the cell with all good intention. But he no sooner reached the cell than its occupant shouted, "Don't come any nearer, you sly old fox! I know who you are."

The county clerk turned instantly, and walked away, saying, "Carry on, Sheriff, carry on."

But the poor man had to go to the mental hospital. A deputy drove the car and the sheriff sat in the back seat with the patient. They chatted and visited until the man was quite comfortable with his situation.

After a time, he asked, "Say, Sheriff, where are we going?"

"Well, I'll tell you," the sheriff answered, "we are going to the hospital."

"We are? Well, what's wrong with me?"

True to the Indian's frank way, the sheriff answered, "Well, because you are crazy!"

No shock, no denials, no bristling. The man simply said, "Oh."

The sheriff was a kind and loving man. He always tried to reach any accident scene before the victim's family got there so that he could make sure they didn't see anything that would further traumatize them. He took in five children and made them his family. He loved to walk, and after he was retired, no longer wanted to drive a car, although when he was sheriff, he'd sometimes driven a hundred miles an hour over narrow roads to catch a car that was running whiskey.

Though the sheriff has been gone for some years, he was recently inducted into the Peace Officer's Hall of Fame. He was respected and loved and the family has forever been grateful that he was never forced to kill anyone in the line of duty. He dealt with whiskey cars and murders and all sorts of crimes, using his Cherokee savvy, his physical strength, and his revolver to stop crimes rather than to kill criminals.

Dust lay two inches thick on the road to the creek. Summer was with us and the dust radiated the heat of the midday sun — too hot for my bare feet. By the time I was halfway to the creek my face was red and my toes scorched. I hopped from the shade of one patch of persimmon leaves that hung over the edge of the road to the next.

While I stood stork-like with one foot drawn up to cool, I saw a hawk flying low over the field across from me and coming directly toward me. Then I saw a furry blur running across the field in zigzags — the typical way a rabbit tries to escape. At first, I thought the hawk did not see the barbed wire fence that edged the field, but it pulled up at the last second, flew in a small smooth circle and came back to light on a fence post.

The rabbit was obviously very tired from running a long way in the intense heat, but she was afraid to stop. Once again, she began running zigzags beneath the fence. When she rounded the fence posts, the hawk darted in, but the barbs held him off. The race was on for another half mile. Finally, they were near the woods and the hawk knew it had failed. As it wheeled away over the trees, the rabbit collapsed where she was and lay panting, gasping for air.

My burning feet were forgotten as I ran down the creek bank, grabbing a huge mulberry leaf as I went. I dipped out a small amount of water and ran back to the rabbit. She was still there, too spent to move. I placed the wet leaf alongside her head, left her and went back to the creek to wait until the road had cooled enough to go home.

The rabbit knew she had had a close call. I had learned something, too. When problems were hot on my tail, I would need to work as hard as I could, zigzag to avoid the claws and look for protection. Grace is always with me. I just need to remember it and not give up.

SPEAK TO ME OF LOVELY THINGS, of treasures yet to be found, of peace that flows like a river. Tell me of tranquil places that no hand has marred, no storm has scarred. Give me visions of standing in the sunlight, or feeling the mist against my cheek as I move and live and breathe.

Show me paths that wind through wild lilies and beds of yellow primroses. Sing me songs of the spheres, the mingled voices of wrens and meadowlarks, the lowing of gentle cows, the soft motherly chuckle of the mare talking to her colt.

Lead me past the glass-smooth pond where frogs croak of their coming-out party, their graduation from frisky tadpoles to squat green frogs that wait patiently for a flying insect.

Find me a place in the sun to sit and think and listen to the sweet inner voice that says so quietly, "Peace. Be still."

THE WOMAN
IN THE MIRROR

SHE OBSERVED HERSELF in the bathroom mirror as she brushed her hair without thought of style or criticism. Suddenly she scrunched her eyebrows in a deep frown and twisted her mouth into a silly grin. She had been making faces in the mirror since she was a child, but now it was so much easier because she had more loose skin to draw into funny faces.

She did not feel her age, but she knew it was considerable because of all the experience she had gathered. Age meant nothing. As the philosophers liked to say, "Age is a state of mind." But she did not think a lot about that either. The other day someone asked her how old she was and she had said casually, "Some days I am eighteen, some days I am 42, some days I am 85 — but I am never my true number of years." At times, she could not recall which age she really was — so she would add twenty-two years to her daughter's age and knew it came close. But most often, she could not recall her daughter's age, and it didn't make any difference anyway.

Today she was going to kick off her shoes and dig in the garden. Doing so was such an uncomplicated thing. Most social activity was simply a way to escape from oneself, she knew. At one time, her Cherokee grandmother had told her to center herself spiritually by putting her bare feet directly on the soil. She said, "Feel the rhythm, sense the pulse of the earth — it is your mother."

After all, the human race came directly or indirectly from the soil — along with growing trees and herbs and medicines from the ground. No creature was put on earth without thought of its comfort or peace of mind, and she was no different. She had known hard times but they served only as molders and shapers to make her who she was — and she was a creation of all her ancients, spiritually and physically.

Once when she was in dire circumstances, sore from worry and hurting in the worst way, she heard a voice. Audible, familiar, friendly, it said to her, "I'll take care of this if you will let me." And she answered, "Yes, Lord, I will let You."

This surrender was not a panacea for all time. Like dipping into a well for a cup of cold water, it had to be done again and again. Thirst does not go away permanently, and neither do problems. But now she knew where the well was and she knew it worked. She could drink whenever she chose — but never without gratitude, never without praise and thanksgiving.

She was an older lady now and had no regrets, no

wishes for youth, no tears for what had or had not happened. She was in the right place. She liked her life simple and without pretense. So what if she had to learn new things that came hard and frustrated her? All she had to do to get back to her center was go to the woods or dig in the dirt. She would never be alone. She turned back to the mirror, made one more homely face, and laughed at her own silliness.

THE PULSE
OF LIFE

MY MOTHER HAS BEEN GONE many years now, but sometimes when the problems of life send my blood pressure soaring, I find she still has much to say to me.

We sit together beneath the broad leaves of the hickory where the ground is bare — because this is where she likes to sit. The ground is Mother Earth and this bare place is her bosom where an ailing spirit is comforted.

She is totally unpretentious, totally comfortable with who she is, and her honesty allows no pretenders to sit with her. Her brown hands with tiny krinkles lie on her calico apron which has a different print from her loose-fitting dress. Her legs are smooth and brown and her feet are in canvas shoes — red ones. They have no strings so that she can get in and out of them easily. Fat braids crisscross the top of her head. Where the hair is black, it is very black, and where it is white, it is silver. A metal bowl of fresh green beans sits on the ground beside her waiting to be snapped when the notion strikes her. But she intends to talk.

"Take off your shoes and put your bare feet on the earth. The pulse of life will rise into your body and your spirit. Don't fidget. Sit quietly and let the Spirit soothe you with its rhythm and its even flow of blood.

"Spirit doesn't have high blood pressure. It has no pressure of any kind. Look up at the leaves moving in the breeze at the top of the tallest tree. No man has ever touched those leaves, but Spirit has. Look at those puffy clouds scudding across the sky — and catch the scent of grapevines blooming. They are out of reach to man — but not to Spirit.

"Answers to your problems seem out of reach to you — but not to Spirit. As a child you were taught that you have spiritual forces — singers and praisers that go out ahead of you to prepare the way. Where have you let them drift to?"

She picks up the bowl of beans and her brown fingers work quickly snapping and tossing. I know she has given me the wisdom I need. It will take a day or two for my mind to form the answers. Meanwhile, I will sing songs of praise. Answers will come, because Spirit never fails.

WINTER
IS OVER

WHEN THAT FEELING OF FREEDOM and lightness enters my heart, I know winter is over. It is time for flowers to appear on the earth. Singing birds and the voice of the turtledove are heard in the land.

Everything old is new again where there is love and beauty. I have scars from past encounters; I am weary in mind and spirit. But when I sing a new song I wash away old hurts that have kept me from going forward. I can still recall the events that hurt me, that shook my soul to its very depths, but those hurts can no longer hold me in their power.

Renewal and restoration began the minute I heard the voice of the turtledove. A saving grace raised me from hell to my knees and then set me back on my feet again. Once I have risen, winter has run its course. My spirit sings and soars with the birds.

What was once frozen and dead within me has dissipated, and spring breaks forth like a stream that thaws and gushes and washes away anything unlike the nature of God. Early rain dissolves the hurt, and later rain purifies and frees the new life within me. It speaks with the voice of the turtledove through a land that stretches far and wide in my heart.

Winter has passed. The rain is over, and flowers appear on earth. I have a new song, a new identity, a new miracle.

WE ARE FRIENDS
FOREVER

MOTHERS OF GRADUATING STUDENTS and the
students themselves worked tirelessly, banking the
school stage with homegrown peonies, roses, honey-
suckle, and anything else that could be brought in to
make this ceremony a memorable time. The scent of
flowers hung in the air as we practiced walking
demurely up long aisles to the stage where we would
get our diplomas. Some would go away to school. Most
of us were without funds to go anywhere.

Many fathers were away fighting a war with
Germany and Japan, and many of our graduates had
already gone to training camps because they became
18 years old before graduation day.

After twelve years together for most of us, the
war was scattering us in all directions and into strange
and unusual experiences. Our innocence was profound.

At eighteen the boys who would soon go off to
war were finally old enough to have their first drink of
beer. They brought it to their private picnic on a pond
dam where they built a fire and started a chicken to

cook over the flames. Then they drank their beer, told stories, laughed, bragged about what their exploits would be. As the beer quickly rose to their heads, the chicken began to have a very appetizing aroma. Wolf was hungry, and suddenly he decided it was time to eat — whether or not the chicken was ready. With all the passing years, there has never been a get-together of our class that someone has not told how Wolf, his thinking and his taste buds dulled by beer, tried to eat a raw chicken gizzard.

Remembering so many nicknames makes a person wonder what we were thinking — Dub, Wolf, Bud, Rat, Egg, to name a few. And there was Earl, who was called Possum, because he would smear black under his nose, comb his straight black hair down over his forehead and goose-step down the aisle — but only when the teacher was turned to the blackboard.

Egg, who was really E. G., owned a big Waltham pocket watch, and when our teacher would turn his back, Egg would put the watch in his mouth and gulp. Only he could do that, because his size would have allowed him to swallow Jonah if the opportunity had afforded itself.

We had so many good memories — corn cob fights at the Wesson Farm, cookouts at the lake, school plays complete with ad-libbing that made even serious drama hilarious. Eugene would never forgive me for the time I gave him Ex-lax and told him it was chocolate.

Basketball was our supreme activity. Mildred could stand in one place and sink a basket that only whispered as it dropped through the net. This feat would take us to the state basketball tournament, and Bill was so excited at her game-winning basket, he yelled, "Ataboy, Mildred!"

Indians make good basketball players — tall and able to guard those six-footers. Alluwe's team had one particularly tall girl, and I was like a bug trying to keep all the other Alluwe players from passing to this butterfly. She was a beautiful girl with long blonde hair and beautiful fair skin — a good player and a fair player, which we could not say for the girls on all the teams we played.

William Cook was our coach and we loved him, but he had a unique accent. It was hard not to laugh when he would yell, "Get thet ball up there and pess it!" (Once, in telling his class news of the war, he said, "Germans threw some bums on a train." Art asked him if they got anything to eat, and was slapped for his humor.)

We girls knew basketball would be our activity for winter, but we had to be creative for summer.

We loved playing tennis at school but at home in summer we had no court, no tennis ball, no net and no rackets. We had nothing but a piece of bare ground, which we cleared in the pasture near the house, and an ordinary rubber ball. We asked the local sawmill for a very thin board and then we proceeded to cut out paddles to use as rackets. The game could hardly be called tennis, but we certainly learned control. If we had not, we would have knocked the ball clear out of the county.

Someone said a new swimming pool had been built up in Kansas so we all got on the streetcar, rode to the end of the line, and walked a mile or two to reach this oasis. Imagine! A place to swim that was not muddy and had no leaches and no poison ivy.

What it did have were cadets from an air base nearby. We hadn't been around many boys, because the war had taken so many of our classmates. Besides, our classmates were like our brothers. The cadets were strange animals. They were men. At the pool we learned to flirt with a glance or a brief smile.

My friend Betty was a "looker," and the cadets all gravitated toward her. However, one went too far when he asked Betty if she was a virgin. She told me what he said and then asked me, "Am I a virgin?" How was I to know? Neither of us knew what the word meant.

The only virgin I'd ever heard about was the Virgin Mary pictured in the Montgomery Ward catalog on the page selling rosaries and statuettes. I recall Mama pointing out to me that these were things Catholics used to worship. She said, "That is not our way." I wondered why not, but it would have been unlikely since there was no Catholic church anywhere near us.

Anyway, Betty sensed this question was off-color and did not get near this fellow again. Cooler weather came, and life changed.

Our circle of friends remained solid. We had no television but we did have what we called "play parties." We sang and danced "Go in and out the Window," which gave the girls and boys a chance to choose someone of the opposite sex to dance around a circle. It was all unbelievably innocent, and would by today's standards be almost ridiculous. But we had real fun nonetheless. Our innocent activities developed our spirits so we could come through wartime, do whatever life demanded, and still show kindness.

Leaving school and leaving the country did not break these solid relationships. We go on, year after year, keeping in touch, being together at least once a year. Genuine love and appreciation is the adhesive that will stand the test of time.

SURPRISING
KINSHIP

I BEGIN MY DAILY JOURNEY INNOCENT of why I have chosen a certain direction. Unconsciously I turn my feet toward a particular hill, or downward toward a free-flowing stream — there where the water is so clear that sun perch can be seen swimming in the sunlight. I like the surprise of finding a new direction, a path untrodden, except for the tiny handprints of the raccoon or the droppings of an elusive doe.

Sometimes I wade the creek with my shoes on, not caring what the leather will do later on. The water swishing around my ankles is like time I have tried to save; it is gone while I am still trying to preserve it.

In my wanderings I come upon a paw-paw tree. When I was a child and found a paw-paw, I wished that it was a banana. Today, I am glad it is a paw-paw. The fruit is elongated and blunt on both ends, as yellow as a banana, but sweet and wonderfully tasty like the tropical papaya.

The paw-paw, growing here in the river bottoms but having kinship to exotic tropical fruits, always seemed to me to be one of those unexplainable links in nature — not so different from the spiritual world where one finds a soul-mate. We recognize this person, not from appearance, but from the spirit. Neither of us know the origins of the other, but it doesn't matter. We know each other from a great distance, and we are only glad the other exists.

We are never so interested in what brought us to this place as we are in what we think and believe now that we are here. Have you thought my thoughts? Do you recognize my spark of life? What does the color "red" mean to you? The figure 8?

Does the dark of night inspire you? Is your mind agile in the morning light? Does the cry of a violin make you weep — not from sorrow but from joy too deep to express?

If I do not see you again this side of heaven, I will know you. I will recognize you from a long way off, because we have a common link, a sweet friendship that disregards time and distance.

It would be no surprise to me if I suddenly waded the creek with my shoes on — just to see you.

On a mutual path, time will telescope and there will not be a time of getting to know each other. We need no proof of our friendship. It is there waiting even before our arrival.

EVEN BEFORE
COMPUTERS

EVERY PERSON who has astounded the world with his brains and intelligence thinks he did it alone. But like mice searching out pieces of cheese by their noses, the human being has simply burrowed in where the spiritual key to all the miracles is hidden. It is hidden within himself.

A group of Indian boys were with the tribal wise man being taught about the life within them — and they, being exposed to the world, asked him if he could work on a computer.

He said, "Oh, yes, I have always had a computer."

The would-be impudent young men looked at each other questioning the sanity of this old man, but, as he spoke, their eyes began to change vision.

"My head and my heart and my belief in the greatest treasure trove, the One God, the Great Holy Spirit Who knows all — this and my willingness to listen and comprehend — are the components of a computer that would occupy a large space were it built in tangible form where you could see it. I am plugged into all Knowledge. None of it is mine alone — but all of it is in neat files for whenever I want to use it."

He looked long at his brown hands, stretching his fingers and moving the muscles in his upper arms, and then he continued, "Should you choose a profession that is in the medical field or teaching or anything that requires your brain and your touch, please remember you are simply God's instrument. You are holy. Your willingness to be taught, to remember, to be humble, will be your greatest gift. By yourself, you are nothing. You are only something when you let yourself be available. Never be overbearing with what you know. It can be jerked away from you in seconds and leave you limp and useless. Always remember where your Power is. Without it, you are a piece of meat with no preservatives."

RECENTLY someone brought me a printout of records down-loaded off the Internet, a transcript of the hearing, sometime before 1900, when my grandfather Arch Sequichie was applying to enroll himself and his two children as citizens by blood of the Cherokee Nation.

In that long-ago hearing, grandfather showed that he was identified on the authenticated roll of 1880 and on the census roll of 1896 as a native Cherokee. He told the commission that he had lived in the Cherokee Nation all his life, and he claimed the right to be listed for enrollment as a Cherokee citizen by blood.

When he filed with the commission properly executed affidavits of the birth of his children, those children would also be listed for enrollment as citizens by blood of the Cherokee Nation.

He would never know that a hundred years later his granddaughter would return to this day and stand beside him in this hearing room to witness the questions they asked him and the intelligent answers of this good man.

Arch Sequichie's reputation still lives among the Western Cherokee people. He was a good man, and he was tough enough to assert himself when it was necessary. As a young man he was sent on horseback to the town of Chelsea to get a doctor for someone who was seriously ill. When he reached the doctor's office he was told that the doctor had gone down to the saloon. He immediately rode to the saloon, but was met at the door by non-Indians and told in no uncertain terms, "No Indians allowed in this saloon. Get going!"

Do you suppose he slunk away and told the sick person those awful men would not let him get to the doctor? No, he loved this kind of challenge. He braced himself and charged through the door like a "bat outta hell," as some observers put it. He busied himself immediately throwing out all the non-Indians — some of them twice. When he finished the job, the doctor invited him to sit down and have a drink before they rode out.

It is well known that Grandfather, his Cherokee /Chickasaw brother-in-law John McIntosh, and his brother Joe Sequichie, who was editor of the first Cherokee newspaper, stood guard on the platform of the Chelsea train station and waited for the train that was carrying black people to the north. Trouble had been threatened if the black folks got off the train in Chelsea. The three Indians, their guns loaded and ready, kept troublemakers at bay so that the people on the train could go inside to eat in peace before they continued their journey.

Grandfather Sequichie played a fiddle — not a cello, but a fiddle. He eventually became a preacher and did all his church services in the Cherokee language. He was a handsome man with coal-black hair and smooth, even features that I saw later in Uncle Carl and in my mother. I only wish that someone had saved his fiddle for me — and some of his talent. I wish I could have known him when he translated Cherokee laws for non-Indian courts. I would have liked to have seen him when he was building roads and culverts and bridges.

Grandfather's sister, Maria Sequichie McIntosh, a graduate of the Female Seminary in Tahlequah, was a tall slender Cherokee lady by whom all social manners of our family were measured. Her husband was Postmaster of Chelsea, and he owned a flour store. Grandfather was not always in her good graces because she said he had not taken advantage of opportunities the way Uncle Joe Sequichie had. He had never earned much money to pass on to his children and grandchildren.

In later years, a woman said my mother was haughty like my Aunt Maria. I disagree. Mama was not haughty but she was stoic. She never saw any reason to talk too much and was never, ever, pretentious.

From Mama I learned that the true worth of a person is never measured by what he or she has, but by who he or she is — in the heart.

Measured by these standards, my grandfather Sequichie left me great inheritance indeed.

LACE,
DIAMOND NECKLACES,
AND MANTELS

AFTER THE STORM, after the stress of drought and heat, and after fear and wonder, came the change of season. As though a door to the treasure room opened to me, I was dazzled with the array of riches, the sparkling, glittering strands of frozen pearls and dew-draped webs like bejeweled scarves with which Earth had covered her head in an act of worship.

The morning sun, freshly polished, broke across the east woods, gently bathing everything it touched. The fence dividing the woods from the red barn was draped in strands of dewy pearls — so many that not even a sheik could afford them. Every blade of grass was covered in hoarfrost and they stood like frozen treats, or elaborate diamond picks to ornament a head of hair dressed for a lord to see.

I stood absolutely still as though it would all disappear if I even batted my eyes.

The sun caught a stretch of dew-covered grass that gave back to my eyes emeralds and topaz and rubies, more wonderful than any person could hope to possess. The jewels we do possess we tend to lock away for safekeeping and no one else can ever see them. What I saw could not be locked away. It would quickly disappear, and yet I know it is mine forever. It comes to me in my soul's memory, and it will come again on the earth in another year, with another change of season.

Beauty like this heals the soul. It is so awesome and so unearthly that we cannot help but know there is more to life than what we see. Materiality flees in the presence of such gifts of spirit. Desire for "things" seems so very unreasonable when I already own this world of treasure. I ask myself, what do I do now? What could top this? What could I dare want when I have had the best and the most extravagantly beautiful?

This beauty is made of the most basic things, light and soil, air and water — things I take for granted. The call of the night bird, the hoot of an owl, the sound of a beloved voice, these become my treasures when I appreciate them.

I am part of a continual celebration. I have no crystal flute of expensive champagne but something better — a drink of life.

LEAVING THE INDIAN LAND where I grew up was not easy. I never would have done it under normal circumstances. But these were not normal circumstances. These were times of war.

I had just finished high school. Papa was away with the army and money was scarce. A department store in Coffeyville, Kansas, just across the state line, offered me a saleslady job and I accepted it eagerly. But how was I to travel to the job? We had no car, but I did have my horse. Mr. Matachek, on the ranch next to our Indian land, owned a saddle shop in Coffeyville. He told me I could ride with him to Delaware, where we would get on the streetcar and go into Kansas. But first I had to get to the neighbor's ranch.

I would ride Figger over to Mr. Matachek's place and tie the horse where my mother could get him during the day. Then I would get into Mr. Matachek's pickup and ride to Delaware where we took the trolley to Coffeyville. The same trip in reverse got me back to the Matacheks' where I took the long walk home across the prairie. As I trudged home, I would be so tired I could hardly lift my feet over the clumps of prairie grass. I would be starved, thinking about what Mama would be cooking for supper. My budget gave me fifteen cents a day for lunch, and since I was a country girl with a good appetite, it was never enough.

One morning when I was dead tired, I did not hear the alarm and I overslept. We had no telephone to call my employer — and he immediately sent word that I was fired. I had never been fired before and it made little impression. But then one of my legs began to swell and that did impress us. The county nurse took one look and told me I had to go to a doctor. The doctor told me I had poison from bad tonsils affecting my leg. The leg had been fractured at one time and had never been set, so a cast was put on my leg. Then, without so much as a blood test to see what my blood count was, the doctor removed my tonsils. I hemorrhaged over and over. An entire summer went by before I was well again, and Mama decided we had better move into town so that I could work without so much hardship.

We left the beloved Indian land with its hills and trees and rocks and moved where we had running water and electricity. The land still belongs to us. The hills are still mine but the house and barn are gone — except in my heart where I can visit them whenever I choose. I still hear the night bird sing, and the crickets and locusts that hummed still call me home.

HOW
TO BE RICH

INVITE THE VISION that will make you rich. Ask for the miraculous ability to see beyond things that rust and corrode and are eaten by moths. Become a receptacle to hold the gifts of life — real life. Stop worshiping possessions — the things that look good, make other people jealous and put everyone on edge.

Use every stalled minute to enjoy Earth's treasure trove, to give sincere thanks for blessings more wonderful than anything human hands can fashion.

One day as I was praying about a problem a rainstorm came though. As it passed, sun rays broke through the clouds to form a small rainbow with one end on my lawn and the other in the ivy bed near the kitchen door. I looked at it in wonderment because it was telling me what I was praying about was already taken care of — and all I had to do was to be thankful.

Another time I had asked in prayer how light could emanate from the Creator enough to light all of the heavens. As I sat in a lawn chair I looked through the kitchen door into the dining room where I had a cut-glass vase sitting on a window sill. The sunrays suddenly touched it, and from the top where it was cut light shot out in every direction — light more bright than a spotlight. The darting light kept playing off the vase in a light show that lasted for many minutes, much like a handful of extremely bright, colorful sparklers.

Some would say that I had a flamboyant imagination. I don't mind. Let them think I have notions of things that never were. But what a pity it is that they do not see the beauty that is everywhere, more real than diamonds and rubies that people so cherish.

It reminds me of what the Sioux Chief said when the tribe was watching the white men take riches out of the Black Hills. "The whites think they are getting rich by digging in the hills, but the Sioux are rich from looking at the hills."

DEEP, DARK, AND LOVELY WOODS

THE FIRST TIME I SAW THESE WOODS I knew this was not just another grove with Sunday afternoon footpaths. It was obviously a haven, a hushed green-tinted hideaway for humans and wild animals.

Deep ravines cut by some immense long-ago force held huge boulders that slid from their moorings in the soft sides of rain-washed earth. Trees of tremendous heights knit together their top branches into a mesh ceiling that let in only dappled sunlight — and made this a deep, dark, and lovely woods.

The tall fronds of woodland fern flourished alongside mayapple and moss-covered stumps of fallen trees. Grapevines with many arms entwined were draped throughout the dense interior. The filtered sunlight haloed in ancient oaks, giving the glow of a massive cathedral with stained glass windows.

After groping one way and then another, I came out in a smaller ravine and stepped into water trickling over gravel and matted ground cover. It was easy to find the source as I could hear the splat, splat, of water dripping from the face of a steep sandstone bluff, and on down to a tiny spring.

Ferns grew in every crevice. Water seeped from the sandstone strata in tiny rivulets to fall on the broad leaves of redbud seedlings that crowded the spring. Tiny, shade-loving yellow flowers bloomed profusely in the deep loam built up over many years of decaying leaves. The outflow of the spring was diminished by sticks and debris that washed against the spillway — until I knelt and scooped out great bunches of black leaves that had rotted in the bottom. At once, the water riled into a dark murky hole, and then settled slowly as fresh water dripped in.

Now our home is in these woods and our wild zoo comes and goes — herds of deer, flocks of wild turkey, coyotes singing evening songs, and rock chucks. We have even seen evidence of a cougar. All these come to the woods to drink from the spring.

I have found that I am like that spring, fresh and sweet in the beginning. With time, I collect debris; invasive plants crowd into my space until I cannot flow. But when I begin to rid myself of all things superfluous, my life is renewed and restored so that I manage more gracefully than ever before.

THE SONG
AND THE VISION

IT WAS A NIGHT WHEN NIGHTINGALES WING through the dark and mysterious wood. Seb and I sat motionless on the roots of ancient trees and watched the moon rise silently over the far mountain range. The view was breathtakingly beautiful and as we sat there a feeling of expectancy and inner sweetness made my heart joyful.

Seb began to sing in his sweet tenor voice and the music drifted out into the moonlit night. As he sang, the angels seemed to fill in the background music. I listened, awed. Then, as the song proceeded, a figure made completely of light came and sat on the air in front of us. Seb continued to sing, and after a few moments the figure beckoned us to come.

Seb stopped singing and the figure disappeared. He began to sing again, and the figure reappeared, again beckoning.

As long as Seb sang the figure was in view, but when the singing stopped, the figure vanished. The song had to be. It seemed the spirit was inhabiting the music — that the song gave it form. This spirit of the night was asking us to follow, and so we did. I joined the singing and we quickly followed the bright figure through an opening in the trees. We emerged into a garden full of fragrant white flowers. The garden was edged with trees through which a brook ran fresh and sweet.

We came into the garden with uplifted hearts and saw a feast prepared for us. The food smelled wonderful — the savory smells that gave us hunger we had not felt. This was to be a night of celebration, a time when music came in waves across the velvet grass.

The dream vision has never been lost to my spirit, but always waits to live again summoned by the song. All I have to do is sing. The song had to be. Even now, the song must be.

LESSONS
WELL LEARNED

As we left the post office, my mother took my hand as though I was still a small child who needed protection from traffic. I was not a child, but a very grown-up-feeling young lady in her late teens.

We crossed Maple Street and walked east along a downhill sidewalk that passed a funeral home, an insurance office, a confectionery, until we came to the great gray south wall of the First National Bank. It was here that I felt our pace slowing, and when I turned to see what she was doing, I was appalled. My mother was about to speak to a known prostitute right under the noses of townspeople.

Mama's warmth was usual and her manner friendly as she chatted amiably with the woman of sad eyes and jet-black hair. Then, as we started in the direction of the grocery store, I whispered in embarrassed tones, "Don't you know she is a prostitute?"

Mama didn't miss a step, but after a short distance she turned to me and said quietly, "She was in my school and her life was very difficult. She was simply a poor little country girl that no one cared about.

No one guided her and no one helped her find the right way." We walked another few steps and she added, "We don't know how she got to this place, we only know she is a human with feelings, and it never hurts to be kind. Beyond that, it is not our place to judge."

I have never forgotten this lesson in grace, which I learned at my mama's side.

NINETY-SIX
AND HOLDING

AFTER SOME ZEALOUS BADGERING I discovered she is 96 years old. She claims she reached that number of years by refusing to form any opinions or make any judgments, but several hours later she had expressed quite a few opinions, including her belief that age is a state of mind.

"The human race is so snagged on staying young they fall into the same trap that Job spoke of when he said, 'The thing I feared has come upon me.' Certainly, I think fear draws to us the very things we fear. I have always been thankful that I discovered that early. It would be a shame to spend one's life being afraid of everything.

"Well, the way I escape that trap is to refuse to accept it. I tell whatever I don't like to get gone — be off!" And she continued rocking gently. Although she was sitting in a rocking chair, I never had the sense that the rocking chair was a sign of her age.

I would have said she was in her late seventies. Her dark skin was barely wrinkled and her hands that lay in her lap were strong and smooth and flexible. They had character, and I had the feeling they had witnessed a lot of life — like the years that ring the old oak tree.

"No, I have never had a facelift — at least not a surgical one — though I have had many mental ones. Those of the mind and spirit are so much easier on you and they benefit more than just the face. However, if there had been a time when I felt I needed a facelift, I would not have hesitated. It is just that I found a better way. You see, I like being who I am. It is not an egotistical thing, you know. It is simply that I recognize my divine right to be who I am and I take care of myself.

"No, I don't spend long hours with other people. I like them — even love a few — but I agree with the proverb that says not to be one of those who drifts from house to house like busybodies. I don't need any of that 'woe is.' I am in no way a loner, but I do like my privacy, and I like other people to have theirs. For myself, sitting at a bridge table is such a loss of time — and there's too much talk, too much hearsay and gossip. Who cares who has sold his house, and his wife only dead a few months.

"Women's Liberation? How should I know. I have never been anything else but a liberated woman. It doesn't take a genius to see success comes on an individual basis. Besides that — listen! — besides that, there is no 'good ole girl' benefit. Men have a working 'good ole boy' arrangement but the time comes when one woman will step in front of another if she is blocking her way. A loyal friend is rare, even among mothers and daughters."

She sat sipping a cup of tea and her eyes wandered to the porch railing where a thick growth of holly-hocks bloomed in pinks and reds. She smiled and asked, "Don't you love the pinks? Keep those colors in your mind and spirit to ward off doldrums and self-pity and the thought that age is an enemy."

"Marriage? Certainly! I did it twice. The first one must have been for practice. I can't think what else it was for — or maybe it was to teach that there is a time to give up. The King in Alice in Wonderland said, 'Begin at the beginning and go on until you come to the end. Then stop.' Too many couples hang on for the sake of the children which does harm. And stop sleeping together without love. It is more the original profession than it is true marriage.

"Of course I don't swear!" Her eyes twinkled merrily, and then she added, "But I know how. I had an uncle who made swearing sound perfectly normal. Oh, it was not vulgar. Vulgarity is ignorance and makes people look gross. They think, I have the right to say what I want, but we all have the right to make ourselves ugly."

To say I was astonished when she answered my

question puts it mildly. "What have I been thinking about? Connections, Honey, connections!"

"Have you noticed how it makes a difference what you are connected to? Have you not noticed how many people think something is looking after them so they can cruise through life without a notion about their destination? Suddenly, they are gone and we wonder if they just fell off the edge of the world.

"We are all like a string of pearls, side by side. We are worn by life — some of us are gleaming with happiness, and some are dull and lusterless. But we have connections with the Maker of Life, and He polishes us as much as we will allow.

"So much of the time we lay claim to helplessness, but we are not helpless. We just want to seem so and go on doing what we want to do without having a good excuse.

"If you are not connected to the right things, my dear, pull the plug! And then reattach where the gold is. It is said that the streets of heaven are paved with transparent gold.

"Let's go for a walk!"

OLD WOODS, NEW TREES

SMALL SEEDLINGS CLUSTER around some of the older trees, giving us a hint that in a few years they will replace the old ones. These are very old woods with many trees that are well over a hundred years old. What tales they could tell about wild animals and humans that once shared this place.

We are those who are replacing our ancients here.

These spreading oaks have a tinge of green in early morning mists. And the shadows are tinted blue like the gauzy curtain of mist that hangs everywhere. Here, the wild rose has turned green and then gray and back to green many times.

This is a comforting place to rest and think. Its invitation is always extended to us to sit quietly here, watching the hawk sail along the air currents, watching the slow-moving clouds float and vaporize and float again.

Along with Standing Bear, we say, "My friends, if you took me away from this land it would be very hard on me."

NO TIME LIKE THIS —
NO END OF THE ROAD

TIME IS SHAPED LIKE A FUNNEL — if it has a shape. Childhood was the large part of the funnel, and as time moves on the funnel narrows and everything moves faster. But time does not bring the end of anything. Life is forever. It just seems that Monday this week got here faster than it did last week.

Those people I no longer see have gone into another room, but they have not ceased to exist. We get to choose which room we want to enter — the one with flowering chestnut trees and crystal-clear streams or some other that none of us want.

We are preparing ourselves now for a life that is better or worse at the next stage. When we have done it all and seen it all, we do not fall off the edge of the world. We live. So this means we are in the moving mode and it is wise to be aware of what to pack. Are we standing for the senseless or do we have faith in a God that already knows what we have in our travel bag?

When life has been so beautiful, why spend any of it in ugly places? Are we supporting right or wrong? Are we denying the truth for what we think is benefiting us? My friends, Truth will always win.

OLD CROOKED LEG had lain on his sick bed for many days and was growing weaker with every hour. His woman of many years sat beside him, her head bowed next to his shoulder. Sons and daughters waited at his feet and tribal members hovered outside the entrance for word of how things were going. Fearful tears were wept silently and a soft chant floated up from the Long House.

Women came to wipe his brow and to give him food — but he was not aware of these quiet efforts. He had not eaten or had water in some time, and few believed he would make it through the night. An occasional cry broke from those gathered around the shelter — and then the moon eased from behind moving clouds and bathed everything in long shadows. An owl hooted. People stirred and wondered, "Is this the end?"

Everything fell quiet. Not a sound, not a twig was broken beneath a moccasin. Old Crooked Leg had paid his dues and everything bowed to him. He had been injured in childhood, his leg had grown crooked, and he had always had trouble walking easily. Even so, he had been a good and faithful chief and was known among all tribes for his wisdom and compassion.

Suddenly through the stillness came a burst of song from the throat of a mockingbird that could not hold its joy until daylight. In that moment, everything changed.

Old Crooked Leg lifted a bronzed hand to his wife, slowly opened his eyes and asked for water. Could this be an apparition? she wondered. Her husband's leg was straight and his toes pointed the way they were created to be. But it was real. "I woke just as the night bird sang," the chief later told her, "and I knew in that hour I was healed."